W9-CQO-417

Building for Tomorrow

Martin Pawley

BUILDING FOR TOMORROW

Putting Waste to Work

Sierra Club Books   San Francisco

The Sierra Club, founded in 1892 by John Muir, has devoted itself to the study and protection of the earth's scenic and ecological resources — mountains, wetlands, woodlands, wild shores and rivers, deserts and plains. The publishing program of the Sierra Club offers books to the public as a nonprofit educational service in the hope that they may enlarge the public's understanding of the Club's basic concerns. The point of view expressed in each book, however, does not necessarily represent that of the Club. The Sierra Club has some fifty chapters coast to coast, in Canada, Hawaii, and Alaska. For information about how you may participate in its programs to preserve wilderness and the quality of life, please address inquiries to Sierra Club, 530 Bush Street, San Francisco, CA 94108.

Library of Congress Cataloging in Publication Data

Pawley, Martin.
Building for tomorrow.

Bibliography: p.
Includes index.
1. Recycling (Waste, etc.) 2. Building materials. I. Title.
TD794.5.P385   333.7   82-5821
ISBN 0-87156-324-X   AACR2

Book design by Jon Goodchild

Printed in the United States of America

10 9 8 7 6 5 4 3 2 1

For Wislard and Bim

Contents

Acknowledgments

Many people played a part in the genesis of this book, none more importantly than Dr. Dora Crouch, who commissioned the small house built of consumer wastes that stood on the Rensselaer Polytechnic Institute (RPI) campus in Troy, New York, from April 1976 to October 1978; that house is the subject of the first chapter. Herb Hirschland, then senior vice-president of research and development of the American Can Company, gave important practical help and advice, as did Smith M. Johnston of the Pawling Rubber Company, Pawling, New York. Patrick Quinn, then dean of the School of Architecture at RPI, and David Haviland, then assistant dean, also gave support without which the project would have been impossible.

The sixteen RPI students who worked on garbage housing (as it was then called) in 1975 and 1976 are credited in the body of the text, but Larry Birch, who was one of them, later helped me run the Experimental Low-Cost Construction Unit at Florida A&M University and took it over after I left. Dean Richard Chalmers, who started

the School of Architecture at Florida A&M in 1975, gave unstinting help in getting this unorthodox master's program off the ground in 1977 and thereafter. Academic Vice-Chancellor Gertrude Simmons was also most helpful.

Jay Pfeiffer and Mitch McCann, formerly of the Office of Manpower Planning of the state of Florida, helped smooth the way to two research contracts on the experimental use of waste materials to improve the energy efficiency of low-income rural housing in North Florida. Michael Reynolds, of Taos, New Mexico; Witold Rybczynski, of McGill University's Minimum Cost Housing Unit; Gernot Minke, director of the Research Laboratory of Experimental Building at the Technical University of Kassel, West Germany; Shiu Kay Kan, architect and designer from London; and Pickett Scott of the Glass Container Corporation, Fullerton, California, were all delegates to the First International Conference of Garbage Architects, held in Tallahassee, Florida, in May 1979. Their presentations and comments were of enormous value, as

were those of the moderator, Forrest Wilson.

Of the students who took the EXCON program at Florida A&M, David Hollister, Millard Wright, and Blakeley Bruce later went on aid mission contracts to Somalia to exercise their skills under the direction of Larry Birch, and Alan Wolfe later joined the faculty. All of them did pioneering work on the development of building techniques for waste materials. Finally, I must thank Dolores Hayden and Peter Marris for a most enjoyable year when I was visiting professor at the School of Urban Planning, UCLA, where most of the survey reading and theorizing evident in these pages took place. To all of these, and to others whose names I may have forgotten, my thanks are due.

Introduction

In the spring of 1973 Chicago sheriff's deputies were called to evict two tenants for nonpayment of rent from a suburban duplex in the old neighborhood of Arlington Heights. They had to break into the house because nobody was there. Inside they found 335 cubic yards of bottles, cans, cartons, paper, food scraps, and other garbage accumulated over thirteen years by an old woman and her daughter. The disposal company given the job of clearing the house said that the quantity removed was ten times more than they collected on a normal round of three hundred houses. "I've never seen anything like it in fifty years in the disposal service," said the owner of the company, according to the *Chicago Sun-Times;* "two of my men got deathly sick and ran out back vomiting."

A few days later, on May 2, a thousand or so miles away, the *Denver Post* featured a large, colored photograph on its front page. It showed a long-haired man in a plaid shirt and a headband holding one of a number of bundles of old beer cans wired together into blocks. "Michael Reynolds, a Taos, N.M., architect-contractor works on a wall of his modern house," read the caption, "built with discarded beverage cans."

Because newspapers picked up both these stories, we know they interested a lot of people. One was the kind that holds a grisly fascination — wallowing in waste — an inkling of the fate threatening all of us. The other was an upbeat ecological counterattack — Yankee ingenuity ain't dead yet. Both were tiny atoms in the endless universe of media stories about the waste problem: a problem that everyone knows about because they are part of it, as are the newspapers themselves.

The trash taken out of the Arlington Heights duplex went straight to the city dump. The 70,000 cans used to build Michael Reynolds' first can house are still in its walls, holding up the roof. When the first owner of the house, a lawyer, came to sell it, he made the usual tidy profit. Subsequent owners have also made profits partly because Michael Reynolds is a gifted architect in the native American tradition of Frank Lloyd Wright, Bruce Goff, and Herb Green and partly because the unusual materials of which the house was made had no negative effect on its mortgagability.

Both the duplex and the can house are important in considering the question of waste — the latter because it showed how at least some kinds of waste could be converted into capital by building and the former because it showed how some other kinds of waste must be processed or transformed by continuous chains of use if they are not finally to exterminate all of us. The cause of waste is processes acting by and for themselves, without awareness of other processes upstream, downstream, or alongside. It is as common in nature as it is in human settlements and is the cause of life as often as it is the cause of pollution. The solution to the crisis of waste is processes interacting with one another, aware of what is upstream, downstream, or alongside. In a man-made world such awareness can only take the form of input-output connections between what are now separate and distinct industries and activities. It is because America grew up through the marvelous energy of an economic system that strove to minimize such connections that it can find no one to make them now.

This book is an attempt to look at the whole issue of waste, particularly the waste generated by the consumer sector, as though it were a natural resource to be pressed into some economic function. This task — to find an economically viable job that it can do — is the most difficult that waste presents, more difficult by far than finding ways to burn it, bury it, or ignore it. Because of this difficulty, the task has been attempted in modern times only under the pressure of irresistible necessity, the kind of crisis of which the recent intimations of energy famine were but a weak example. Before the gasoline lines of 1974 there was the rubber crisis of 1942; and apart from the United States there have been other countries at war whose struggles with resource starvation were ultimately lost. In those countries, under desperate necessity, waste was virtually eliminated — but only in the context of the general waste that is war itself. For Americans before 1942 there was the the poverty of the depression, and before that the war of 1917 and the war of 1861 and earlier wars, all of them focusing suddenly on the enormous cost of waste. Despite the ironic context, recent wars offer many examples of ingenuity in the avoidance or utilization of waste.

Nature, too, while she is prolific with waste, also resolves the problems it creates with breath-taking ingenuity. If we compare our machines and processes with those existing in nature, we see in the whole drama of evolution an extraordinarily complex and sophisticated pattern of interactions, with exploitive and supportive interfaces between species that consume and reuse every waste crumb of food, every redundant movement and sensory limitation. With the coming of biotechnology, the concept of harnessing the power of heredity as a productive force, we may find ways to control and exploit man-made waste by these genetic methods.

In this book, more than warfare and the natural world, the main area considered is construction and in particular the use of waste buildings in a future economy. Recent energy studies and surveys of possible uses for agricultural and industrial wastes in construction provide a rich resource here but only within the context of a conventional construction industry developing along conventional lines. Material substitutions such as crushed glass aggregates, waste rock ballast, or rice-hull-based fireproof doors have been experimentally used already. But the simple, intuitive notion of secondary use is underregarded, and the idea of buildings themselves as storage systems for resources has not yet been framed. The potential of construction for the absorption of waste in the future is everywhere agreed, but the idea that the whole resource base of the industry might change in pursuit of this aim is still a dream.

Building for Tomorrow is an attempt to look at the potential of waste from these three standpoints. It is another book about waste in America, but it is not a doomsday book, a book about bottle laws or recycling programs, or a book about what you should urge your community to do. It is a book founded on a heresy, the idea that there is nothing unnatural about massive overproduction, high levels of waste, and marginal survival — all of which are as much characteristics of the natural world as of our own industrial society. From this position flows the notion that our waste products, and the products that become waste because of their volume, production, and short life, must be disposable through some such system of cycles of decomposition and reproduction, commensalism, mutualism, and parasitism, as enables the natural world to maintain high energy flows without ruinously short-term economics. Whether design and construction could play as large a part in this process as the author believes is for the reader to decide.

Martin Pawley,
Torcross, March 1981

1 A House for $501.70

" Troy, N.Y., April 8 (AP) — The house may be small and constructed in less than a month out of sheer trash. But the view is great, and the buyer is eager. Seven architecture students at the Rensselaer Polytechnic Institute are building the house from tin cans, cardboard tubes from newsprint rolls, 16-ounce beverage bottles, and metal strapping used in packaging as a class project in cheap construction. A professor bought it for $600 before the first beer bottle went up. "

New York Daily News, April 9, 1976

A House for $501.70

The first building experiments we tried at the School of Architecture, Rensselaer Polytechnic Institute, were based on the waste materials that came most easily to hand. We used cans from campus food outlets, bottles, scrap steel strapping from Star Textiles at Cohoes (which we tensioned and cut with a $21 German tool called the *Klammer*), and, last but not least, the 4-inch-diameter heavy tubes of cardboard used as centering for the rolls of newsprint consumed by the local newspaper. Later on, we were given 4,000 No. 10 catering cans by the American Can Company, and, because these did not require cleaning before use, they saved us a lot of time when we came to build the house. We never did find a use for the 10,000 off-grade billiard balls thrown away every week by an Albany plastics company or the 40 tons of weak asbestos cement trucked daily to a landfill from the Bendix brake lining plant on nearby Green Island.

Our earliest structures were little more than sheds built from the exotic materials we collected. One consisted of steel cans braized together with an acetylene torch; the other was the first to be built using the newsprint cores as framing. Finished just before Christmas 1975 with a black-polyethylene-covered roof and tarred cardboard walls, this modest structure served the local subteen population as a kind of clubhouse until they discovered (perhaps by accident) just how flammable it was. On March 15, 1976, under the horrified gaze of students, faculty, and campus police, the "tube house" was consumed by fire.

However unsuccessful these earliest experiments might have seemed (the small "can house" was also pulverized by vandals in due course), their extremely low cost as buildings had already occasioned comment. There had, of course, been no paid labor on either project, but as a result of the use of very common wastes the material cost of each had been about a dime a square foot at a time when conventional house construction was running at $25 or more. Furthermore, as I tirelessly proclaimed, our patient searches for material suppliers had uncovered enough for a hundred such structures without moving more than a couple of miles from the center of the campus. Every week the *Troy Times-Record* dumped 150 newsprint cores in sizes ranging from 60 inches to 28 inches in length, and we used only forty to make a roof truss capable of covering 60 square feet. In the early weeks of 1976 we improved on this by developing a "stretched" truss spanning 16 feet, which, with a spacer section either side of it, could cover 200 square feet of floor space with only sixty tubes.

The supply situation with other wastes was equally promising. The Rensselaer food outlets on campus generated about 600 No. 5 and No. 10 cans every week. Steel strapping was being thrown away by Star Textiles

1. One of the two predecessors to the Dora Crouch house, the can structure designed and built by Al Lagocki, Roy Hall, Robin Rakusin, and Joleen Boody in the fall of 1975. This 150-square-foot enclosure was built from 2,200 No. 10 cans collected from campus food outlets and brazed together using an acetylene torch. The roof (snow-covered in the photograph) was formed from No. 10 cans opened out into half figure-eight-shaped tiles. The roller door was formed from No. 5 cans brazed to scrap steel strapping. The missing bottle infill to the right of the door is evidence of early vandalism.

of Cohoes in 600-pound bales. One of these lasted us a whole year and prompted us to beg money from the school to buy a $90 strapping tool that worked better and faster than the *Klammer* because it used cheap metal seals instead of heavy steel buckles to join the sections of ⅝-inch steel strap. Bottles were never a problem. In fact, as time passed, the supply increased largely because most people seem to keep them through inertia until they have a station wagon load.

In the course of my teaching duties I had many opportunities to extol the virtues of waste and assert that therein lay the solution to the housing problem. At the time I believed that the house price spiral was destined to end on a plateau of equity where no one could afford to buy without fifteen cosigners and no one could afford to sell without giving away half his or her imaginary gains. At such a point, I thought, the simple 10-cents-a-square-foot house would come into its own. It was probably this sort of talk that lured Dora Crouch into the small group of garbage enthusiasts. She had joined the RPI faculty the year before I arrived, coming from the West Coast with three children, two of whom were about to enter college and were thus in need of low-cost accommodation. Why not, she ingeniously thought, have my students and I build a full-size garbage house in which her children could live while they went to college? She calculated that the cost, even at ten times my outrageous prices, would be on the order of two months rent for her own faculty apartment. If the house could be built on campus as an experiment, she would soon recoup her investment; if the operation was a total failure, the loss would not be catastrophic.

At the time, snow lay deep on the ground, and my students were working in a fourth floor studio designing, building, and testing to destruction full-size garbage flooring systems capable of complying with New York State building codes.[1] All of these structures, some of them upward of 30 feet long, were impossible to remove from the building intact, and the steady increase in their number was already creating friction between those engaged in put-up-or-shut-up garbage experiments and those sweating away at the more usual school of architecture chores — opera houses, resort villages, and town halls. The chance to put up a real building when the weather broke was too good to miss. Furthermore, the authorities seemed surprisingly enthusiastic about the project and donated a site on the eastern edge of the campus. The director of facilities planning even persuaded the large building contracting firm at that time erecting a $10 million engineering building at the institute to donate not only a concrete ground slab for the house but also a mortar mixer for as long as we needed it.[2]

At the beginning of March 1976 Dora Crouch opened a "Garbage House Account" at the campus branch of the Marine Midland Bank and deposited $600. Now the only thing to do was to design and build it.

Owing to the structure of the curriculum, the six students who signed up for the garbage housing course that spring were not the ones who had worked on the smaller structures in the fall, and this fact soon became evident. The first design competition for the house ended in acrimony, with my denouncing each project as more hopelessly ambitious than the last. We had perhaps six weeks to build the shell of the house before the long summer vacation. In my view, we could not include any solar, wind, or other unconventional energy systems, nor could we even think of going up to two stories for lack of scaffolding or other equipment. Because a client's money was at stake, only tried and tested methods could be used. After much argument, it became clear that the choice was between a larger and improved version of the "tube house," which had not yet burned down, or turning down the job. In the end the challenge of building the house won.

From this point on, there was no time to lose. In the atmosphere of mounting excitement generated by approval of the project, even a twelve-point objection to the idea from the institute's legal department ("another aspect of this construction that we should look into is its effect on labor unions in the area") failed to slow us down. A quick drawing of a 34-foot by 17-foot reinforced concrete slab with a plumbing knock-out in one corner was sent to the contractor, and by the third week in March the concrete pad for the house was in position.

The Dora Crouch House

Floor plan

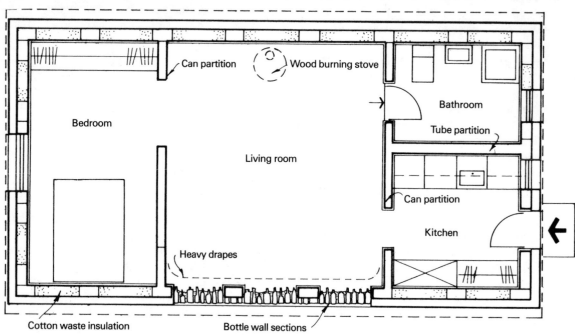

Can partition

Wood burning stove

Bedroom

Living room

Bathroom

Tube partition

Can partition

Kitchen

Heavy drapes

2.

Cotton waste insulation

Bottle wall sections

Section

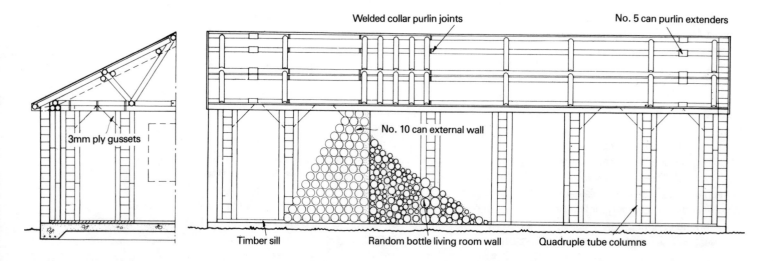

3mm ply gussets

Welded collar purlin joints

No. 5 can purlin extenders

No. 10 can external wall

Timber sill

Random bottle living room wall

Quadruple tube columns

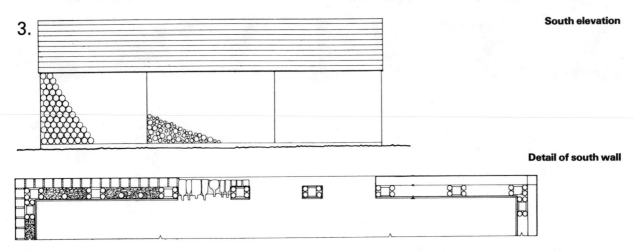

3.

South elevation

Detail of south wall

The design of the house was simple in the extreme. There was only one door, one window for the kitchen (which doubled as an entrance hall), another window for the bathroom, and a third in the bedroom, which ran the full width of the west end of the 500-square-foot dwelling. The central living room had no windows as such, but the whole of its south wall was to be glazed from floor to ceiling in bottles of various colors set in cement mortar. The framing of the house was an improvement on the newsprint core columns and trusses developed in the fall. The columns were now four-legged, based on a beam design by student Robert Beck, and triangular masonite gussets were squeezed tight between the legs of the columns and the ring beam of tubes that ran around the house at eaves level to receive the roof trusses. The entire assembly of tubes was based on the geometry of uncut cores, used exactly as they came from the newspaper in 28-inch, 42-inch and 56-inch lengths joined longitudinally with No. 5 steel cans and roofing nails, and butt-jointed with 16-ounce nonreturn beverage bottles with all compression applied with re-used scrap steel strapping. In all, twenty-four four-legged columns were prefabricated at the school before being hauled up to the site where work commenced the first week in April.

With the luxury of a level concrete slab to work from and the constant dimensions of the cardboard tubes themselves to aid accuracy, the frame of the house went up with awe-inspiring speed. No electricity was available, and no power tools were necessary. Nonetheless, required by the institute to wear hard hats on the job, we looked so convincing that the roving builders' chuck wagon driver stopped twice a day without comment — until he read about the garbage house in the paper. At the end of the first week, all the columns and the ring beam were strapped into place, with the feet of the columns securely toe-nailed into the 8-inch by 2-inch wooden sole plate, which was itself plugged down to the concrete. Every 6 feet, long steel straps ran from the top of the ring beam around the sole plate and back. These straps added immensely to the rigidity of the structure, but they resonated so loudly in the wind that conversation became impossible; in the end we wound masking tape around them to keep them quiet.

By the end of the second week we had fabricated three roof trusses and lifted them into position from the slab itself. The last was more difficult as we had to assemble it in a neighboring parking lot and carry it across the road to the house. It weighed 500 pounds and gave more trouble than any of its predecessors. In the end, it had to be torqued into position with the strapping tool pulling 30 feet from one end of the house to the other.

My major concern at this time was rain, for tests had

4. The cardboard newsprint core framing of the house in position prior to locating tube rafters and covering the roof. The four-legged columns can be clearly seen, as can the mode of joining the purlin cores longitudinally, using No. 10 cans in walls, No. 5 cans in trusses and purlins, and roofing nails.

disclosed that the Northern Paper Company cores delaminated when they got truly wet and, worse still, deformed generously along the line of the load applied to them. For this reason, we had begged large supplies of scrap-reinforced plastic sheeting from the benign contractor, and we now proceeded to wrap every part of the exposed structure with it, stapling it into position to prevent the wind from tearing it off. The roof itself was framed in tube "rafters" at 16 inches on center, and these we covered with three layers of waste packaging cardboard held down with roofing nails; this subroof too was covered with plastic sheet.

Some time before, we had decided to use the 4,000 No. 10 cans donated by the American Can Company as an outer cladding for the house, laid like round and shiny bricks in cement mortar, although we were later to rue our failure to explore the possibilities of a sheet material of some kind because "can-laying" proved to be as time consuming as tube construction was quick. The actual roof covering had never been defined. Because the roof of the earlier tube structure, which had been burned before it decayed, was finished with 6-mil black polyethylene, it seemed logical to use this material again even though we knew that the ultraviolet component in sunlight would break it down eventually. The real problem was cost — at least $50 for a roof of our size — and the question of how often would it have to be replaced. For this reason I was overjoyed when my friend Witold Rybczynski, of the McGill University Minimum Cost Housing Group (MCHG), offered to come down and try out a membrane roof made from sulfur and chopped glass fibers painted onto large cardboard "tiles." MCHG had just completed a sulfur building for the Creek Indians at Saddle Lake in Alberta and had also built the walls for a 2,000-square-foot children's welfare building in Quebec from sulfur concrete blocks. By mid-April it was agreed that a team would come down almost immediately to apply the revolutionary roof covering. Our job was to obtain the sulfur they would need.

It was about this time, with the skeleton of the house clearly visible, that the project first began to attract publicity. A story about a dwelling made from newsprint cores would be hard for any newspaper to ignore, but the *Troy Times-Record* managed it, and the nearby *Albany Times-Union* got there first with a picture story that went out on the Associated Press wire service and was picked up all over the country. The picture showed student Debbie Jones wearing a hard hat and carrying a bundle of newsprint cores past the front of the house. Within twenty-four hours Debbie was inundated with fan mail and letters from cranks; a rabbi from Texas blessed her for restoring his faith in the work ethic; and a Southern Baptist assured her she would go to hell. More significant from our point of view was the effect her fame had upon her relatives, one of whom was able to induce American Cyanamid to donate a load of sulfur in 20-pound bags.

The visit by the McGill team lasted for two weeks. Working steadily with electric skillets in an adjacent barn, Witold and his assistant, Bernard Lefebvre, heated the sulfur to 220 degrees Fahrenheit in order to make it liquid, added half-inch chopped-glass fibers and a dash of dicyclopentadiene plasticizer, and painted the dark yellow soup onto large sheets of cardboard cut from discarded furniture boxes. It set rapidly with a hard glaze. When a sufficient number of these "tiles" were ready, they were taken to the roof and nailed down. The nail heads and joints between tiles were painted over with more sulfur and glass fiber, heated up, and applied on the roof itself.

Perhaps because of our elaborate precautions there was not one drop of rain during the roofing period. I remember this well because the first ominous clouds were gathering as the McGill people bade us goodbye and headed north for Montreal, laden with photographs of their pioneering venture. Student Tim Ryan and I stood that evening by the half-completed shell, and in the silence a kind of breakfast-cereal crackling could be heard. "What's that?" I asked. "The roof," he answered. We both visualized billions of cracks appearing in the thin sulfur membrane as the temperature fell, and dismissed the thought as unthinkable.

Next morning I arose unusually early. It had rained heavily all night, and I wanted to see how the roof had

5. With columns bagged in polyethylene for protection from the rain during the construction, part of the cardboard roof covering is already in position. Tube rafters can be seen to the right.

6. Laying No. 10 cans supplied by the American Can Company. The problems caused by not building the corners first can be seen in this photograph, where the right-hand corner is now shuttered in for poured concrete. Later (and less visible) corners were more successful. The figures on the roof are members of the McGill team laying the ill-fated sulfur membrane roof. To the right, the bottle wall is already finished.

worked out. I drove to the site, and before I had even switched off my windshield wipers, I could see that things were worse than my wildest dreams. Whole sections of the sulfur-coated cardboard had buckled and folded back. The rain had filtered through the tiny cracks we had heard forming, caused the cardboard beneath to swell up and make bigger cracks, and thus pulled the whole roof surface apart. Two weeks of work had come to nothing in about twelve hours.

We stripped off the sulfur cardboard piece by piece and piled up the remains. Only the plastic sheet covering the subroof had saved the structural frame of the house from saturation. Glumly, we contemplated a return to short-life polyethylene, and in fact that was how we surfaced the roof that spring. But publicity had something more in store than bags of sulfur.

I had been interviewed on radio about the garbage house, and one broadcast, by John Gambling of WOR in New York City, was heard by Smith Johnson, president of the Pawling Rubber Company of Pawling, New York. Johnson, like most of the older generation of American production men I have met, not only instantly grasped the value of building with waste but connected the idea with something his own company threw away in unavoidably large quantities: 2-foot-by-2-foot sheets of neoprene rubber left in the pressure molding machine after the formation of every 144 bushings for the auto industry. The rubber sheets, sometimes called backplates or mold linings, were about one-fourth of an inch thick and good for 30,000 miles — like the product itself. Smith Johnson immediately saw that these could be used as a kind of flexible roofing tile, and he wrote to me, care of John Gambling.

In early May 1976 this bonanza was still in the future. Johnson's letter was forwarded to RPI but arrived after I had left for the summer vacation, so it played no part in the history of the house until the fall. The completion of the shell that spring took place against a background of term papers and final examinations, which thinned the ranks of the student construction workers with every passing day. There were other setbacks too. A shortcut to can-laying invented by Tim Ryan, which con-

sisted of arranging ten cans in a triangular form and casting them in batches, turned out to be a near disaster. Unlike the sulfur roof, this one had prototyped out perfectly; it was a light, strong, and, most important of all, large building element, three rows of which would reach from slab to eaves. Alas, when we batch-cast thirty of them on the floor of the house, more than half of them broke on lifting, and many of the remainder did not survive handling into position. Clearly, the mortar mix and the curing time were critical, and we had just struck lucky with the first one. In the end only one small section of the outer wall was built using the ten-can blocks; the remainder was done with single cans in mortar.

While speed and media interest had enlivened the task of assembling the tube frame, laying 2,800 cans in mortar by hand was a very different matter, though even this hardly compared with the misery of laying the floor-to-ceiling bottle wall for the living room. Painfully, we discovered for ourselves the importance of organization and skill in what was after all only a variant of masonry construction with none of the ingenious side-steps we had employed on the rest of the house. At first, can-layers drummed their fingers for want of mortar, and mortar mixers dumped barrows of mix because there was nobody to use it. We demonstrated our largely theoretical knowledge of building technology by building the lengths of wall first and the corners last, a disaster that any mason would have avoided and that led to the southwest corner of the house coming together so badly that we were obliged to set up formwork and pour it in solid concrete.

Our only encouragement during this deadline phase was the extraordinary appearance of the house itself. No matter that what we were doing was primitive, the result looked highly professional. The hundreds of steel cans, large shiny circles on the outside, looked as good as milled aluminum on the dashboard of the most expensive hand-built car, for corrosion had as yet barely touched their metallic splendor. The bottles, too, rapidly lost their prosaic appearance and melded into a veritable Chartres Cathedral of stained glass, glistening from within during the day and from outside at night when the interior was lit.

By the last week of the semester, the shell of the house was all but done. Used windows, bought for a few dollars, were built into position as the walls rose, and the roof finally received its covering of transparent polyethylene laid on a glutinous coating of cold tar. The door, painstakingly diagonal boarded by two fashion-conscious students, now opened and closed with a key. A steady stream of visitors, lured from the neighboring fieldhouse parking lot or brought greater distances by television and newspaper publicity, now stood in silence as they contemplated this miraculous structure. One lesson I learned from all those visitors was that the average American — as opposed to the average American intel-

lectual — is not prejudiced against secondary use or houses built from bottles and cans and cardboard. He or she is frequently surprised by the solidity of such a building, but mostly is impressed by the *use* that can be made of things everyone throws away but still, after all this time, hates to waste. As a result of this reaction, the tribute in bottles and cans that we received stepped up as the house progressed. Every day people drove up in their cars and unloaded building materials; every morning we found bags of bottles left by anonymous contributors.

The time came for all involved to depart. Client, architect, and architectural students bade each other farewell. At this stage each had cause to feel satisfaction and anxiety. Dora Crouch was the owner of a 600-square-foot

7. The west end of the house completed before sulfur coating. The roof is covered in cold tar and translucent polyethylene, which preceded the neoprene version and followed the unsuccessful sulfur. Differential corrosion of the steel cans is already visible.

shell (hardly yet a house) for a total expenditure of $501.70[3] It had been featured in sixty-one newspapers reaching over 20 million readers, been shown on many television news programs, and been the subject of numerous radio interviews. But it would be many months before her children could live in it. I myself had become convinced, despite all mistakes and exaggerations, that it was possible to develop a technology to build with wastes *as they are,* instead of processing them into special building materials at giant municipal facilities. In their turn, the students had taken part in a farce that had turned out to be an adventure — the first step on a journey that might lead to a whole new realm of architecture based on resource recovery.

But there were causes for dissatisfaction too. Everyone was convinced by the structure we had erected, but few knew of the sulfur roof fiasco or the poured concrete corners. Few of us even faced the implication of the amount of costly cement that was now going into the once truly garbage house. Then there was the problem of corrosion now gaining prominence with each passing day. Worst of all was the extent of water penetration through the walls in driving rain. All were closely guarded secrets, but for how long?

In any event, no defect in design or construction proved crucial during the three-month period of neglect that followed. In September the house was still intact, but the polyethylene roof covering had all but disappeared: it had broken down under ultraviolet radiation, split, cracked, and blown away. Once again the "insurance" layer of plastic beneath the cold tar had saved the frame beneath. The can walls were now heavily rusted, with the mortar between cans stained with rusty streaks. Inside the house, the results of rain penetration were obvious, with the condition of the lower columns and floor reminiscent of an Egyptian temple flooded by the Nile. The only consolation was that, perhaps because of the altitude of the house above campus and town, vandals had barely touched it. One window was broken as were two or three bottles in the bottle wall, and the door had been forced; that was all.

The fall semester garbage housing team was

smaller than either of its predecessors; the students who had previously taken the course were ineligible for one reason or another to take it again. This time there were only three volunteers: Bruce Hamilton, Ed Wheeler, and Dale Dracup — joined a few days later by Hollee Becker, an engineering student, who took the course as an elective. This enrollment was so small that it appeared unlikely that the course would ever again be offered as a full studio, a judgment that was confirmed by the new attitude the institute authorities took to the project.

There had been, it seemed, an exchange of memoranda between the administration and the client, who had been forcefully disabused of the idea that the house belonged to her. Furthermore, it had been decided that

8. The neoprene rubber roof tile system. The rubber injection press squeezes rubber through 144 small nozzles to produce tiny auto bushings.

15

no one could occupy the house, even as an experiment, because it lacked electricity, water, and sewage connections. We rapidly obtained estimates for making these connections, somewhere in the region of $3,500, because there was hope that the money could be found provided the authorities would agree to occupation in advance. They would not.

Faced with what appeared to be a dead end, Dora regretfully closed the garbage housing account at the bank and prepared to write off the money already spent to experience. The rest of us determined to complete the house as far as possible before Christmas in the hope that it would stand for a number of years even if unused.

Robbed of our budget, we found a strange exhila-

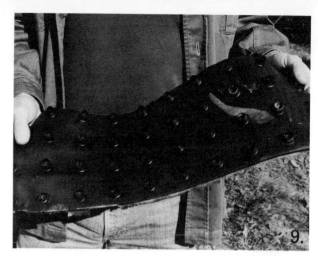

9.

9 and 10. Left in the press after the bushings are formed is a 28-inch by 28-inch layer of rubber about ¼-inch thick. This is the mold lining, or backplate, which is a waste product (9). The roof covering (10) is made from backplates nailed to the roof structure with roofing nails. Because the neoprene closes up around the nails, it is possible to fix from the top as well as the bottom if necessary.

10.

ration in absolute instead of relative poverty. The first thing we did was to visit Smith Johnson in Pawling and bring back two vanloads of the neoprene backplates. These proved to be even better in fact than they had seemed on paper. We nailed them to the roof like shingles, starting at the eaves and ending with the ridge, only to discover that they were so flexible and elastic (the rubber closed around the nail hole to make a water-tight seal) that they could have been nailed through from the top if necessary and still would not have leaked. It would be difficult to imagine a better low-cost roofing material than this waste product. From the day the roof was covered to the day of the house's demolition two years later, the plates never leaked a drop of water.

After fixing the roof, we turned our attention to the walls with their twin problem of rusting and rain penetration. After further consultations with McGill, we decided the remaining sulfur might work as a waterproof coating painted onto the outer surface of the cans and their mortar joints. Soon we too became adept at melting two or three electric skillets full of sulfur at a time, applying the hot, quick-drying liquid to the walls with large bristle brushes. Bruce Hamilton, an artist as well as an architectural student, found ways to use the difference in color between successive sulfur batches to decorative effect. To our great relief, the glaze went on easily and stopped rain penetration immediately. The corrosion of the cans, if not arrested, was at least rendered invisible.

11. The house after sulfur-coating the exterior walls in order to retard corrosion of the steel cans. The final effect was a kind of camouflage pattern in different shades of yellow, caused by different heating times and temperatures.

17

By the middle of October the summertime disintegration of the envelope of the house had been arrested, and we were able to turn our attention to the interior. At last, we arranged a temporary electrical supply and worked late in the evenings to insulate the walls and ceiling with 8-inch thicknesses of cotton polyester from the Cohoes textile company that had previously donated the steel strapping. Inside, we lined the rooms with more of the endlessly available newsprint cores, creating a log cabin effect. We installed an ex-GI wood-burning stove in the living room and, eventually, carpets, chairs, and other items of furniture including a television set and sundry wall decorations. The cardboard tubes were used with increasing skill in a number of new roles: as bunk beds,

closets, and other interior fittings as well as wall linings. In the final phase of occupation, we fitted rain-water gutters with an attached collection system to provide a modest water supply and contemplated but could not afford a chemical toilet to permit clandestine occupation during the coming winter.

Toward the end of the semester the director of security and safety paid us a visit and condemned our temporary electrical installation. Next morning our buried supply cable was disconnected and a seal placed on the receptacle with threats of dire consequences should we attempt to reconnect it. In December in upstate New York, with short days and bitter cold, this was a death sentence on the house. Without electricity we could not

12 and 13. Two interior views showing the extensive use made of the free newsprint cores to provide a wall lining retaining the 8-inches of waste polyester insulation and to create a somewhat log-cabin-like effect. Wood-burning stove and other home comforts are visible (**12**), as is the pleasant effect of the south-facing bottle wall to the living room (**13**).

12.

finish the house, and if it were not usable, it would very soon be vandalized again.

Over the weekend of December 11–12, 1976, the house was broken into and our tools, fittings, stove, and other goods stolen. An exchange of memoranda between myself and the campus police took place, but there was nothing to be done. On December 15 I left Rensselaer Polytechnic Institute at the close of my visit. By the time I passed that way again, in November 1978, the house had been demolished.

The Dora Crouch house was an elementary and unscientific experiment in secondary use construction. Although it stood untended and vandalized for two years, it was structurally sound and, with reasonable maintenance and repair, could have stood for many years if it had not been demolished to make way for a storage facility in October 1978. Its appearance was strange rather than impressive, reflecting the number of alternative ideas tried out on it during construction. A team from the American Can Company, which came to investigate in May 1976, retired without comment, and a proposal to market a truck-mounted can-forming machine for construction sites, about which we had heard, came to nothing. In retrospect, the most remarkable thing about the project was not that it was possible with no experience and very little money to find all the things necessary to build such a house but that it was possible

13.

19

to build a house with all the things that were there, whatever they were.

In 1976 I knew nothing of the houses built by Michael Reynolds in and around Taos, New Mexico, so much more durable and impressive than this modest structure; but by the end of the year I did not know that the resource base of the construction industry *could* be shifted so that it became a kind of waste disposal process in itself. I knew also that the economic and energetic consequences of such a shift could be *evolutionary* in their importance. The rest of this book is about that idea.

Notes

1. In all, sixteen students worked on garbage housing at RPI from September 1975 to December 1976. Ray Weisner, Al Lagocki, Robin Rakusin, Joleen Boody, Grahame Knowland, and Gary Mooring worked on the two small structures completed in the fall semester. The larger task of building the shell of the Dora Crouch house was carried out by Tim Ryan, Bob Beck, Debbie Jones, Marquand Johnson, Dave Capelli, and Scott Stinson. New work to the roof, walls, and the interior of the house in the fall of 1976 was done by Ed Wheeler, Bruce Hamilton, Dale Dracup, and Hollee Becker.

2. Apart from Messrs. Sweet & Company's all-important gift of the concrete ground slab and the mortar mixer, the following businesses were generous with their help on the house. Star Textiles, Cohoes, N.Y., gave strapping and waste cotton polyester; the Pawling Rubber Company, Pawling, N.Y., gave neoprene backplates; the *Troy Times-Record* gave newsprint cores; Standard Furniture Company, Troy, N.Y., was a major source of cardboard; American Cyanamid Corporation gave and delivered 500 pounds of sulfur; and the American Can Company gave 4,000 brand new cans. RPI loaned wheelbarrows, shovels, and hand tools.

3. The final cost of the house was the sum of equipment, material, and transport in the following quantities: $111.82 on hard hats, electric skillets, paintbrushes, mat knives, blades, and gloves; $350.28 on cement and lime, three used windows, nails and screws, styrofoam slab insulation, cold tar, and polyethylene sheets; $39.60 on a new gas tank for the Ford station wagon we used to transport wastes and materials. The actual material cost for the house shell was $330.28 or 55 cents per square foot, but the number of free items makes this figure difficult to compare with conventional construction costs.

2 | Waste in America

" We brush our teeth with fluoride compounds, rub on propylene glycol deodorants, clothe ourselves in rayon and nylon or treated cotton and wool, drive cars filled with the products of a liver carcinogen called vinyl chloride, talk on plastic phones, walk on synthetic tiles, live within walls coated with chemical-laden paint. Our food, kept fresh in refrigerators by heat-absorbent refrigerants, contains preservatives and chemical additives. And of course, it has been grown with the aid of chemical fertilizers and insecticides. The detergents, the medicines, the foam rubber, and the floor cleaners—all have their underside of waste. **"**

Michael Brown, *Laying Waste,* 1980

Waste in America

The continental United States has a fixed area of 2.27 billion acres and an increasing population, so the acreage per person steadily falls.[1] In 1800 it was 450, in 1900 down to 35, in 1970 down again to 11, and by the year 2000 it will be only 7. It is a peculiarity of urbanization in America that this massive population increase has, by and large, been confined to four major corridors, which together only add up to 10 percent of the land area — even though they accommodate 75 percent of the population. They are the Northeast (Boston to Washington, D.C.); the Midwest (Chicago, Cleveland, Pittsburgh); the West (San Francisco to San Diego), and the Southeast (Jacksonville to Miami). Outside these zones of intense development 50 percent of the national area is classified as agricultural land and 30 percent is forest. National parks and wilderness account for 5 percent, landfill sites for 0.02 percent.

Against the background of this broad pattern of land use, the operations of the U.S. economy take place, consuming about 6 billion tons of fuels and raw materials every year in order to produce 300 million tons of food, 250 million tons of major manufactured materials (paper, metals, glass, textiles, plastics, and rubber), and 5 trillion kilowatt-hours of electricity.

Only about 1 percent of the raw materials fed into this vast productive mechanism is retrieved by the resource recovery industry; the remainder is either in current use, in stock against future use, or waste. The last is by far the largest category of the three. As scientifically defined, waste comprises unused heat, gases, airborne or waterborne particles, fluids and aerosols, as well as the more readily identifiable forms generated by industry, commerce, and consumption. Table 1 gives a broad breakdown of the major solid waste sources in the economy.

The inclusion of topsoil loss, which results naturally from wind and water erosion but is accelerated by irrigation, plowing, and cropping, is made here in order to show that waste output in an entropic sense exceeds resource input. If we avoid the problem of distinguishing between natural and man-caused topsoil loss by exclud-

Table 1. Gross Solid Waste Output of the U.S. Economy by Weight

Source	Millions of Tons per Year	Percentage
Topsoil loss	4,000	55
Mining	2,270	31
Agriculture	705	9
Urbanization	180	2.5
Industry	180	2.5
Total	7,335	

ing it altogether, the measurable weight of solid waste drops to just over half the weight of input, and this is perhaps a better indicator of the size of the manageable waste problem.

With 6 billion tons of solid raw material going in, and only 3.3 billion tons of solid waste coming out, the sheer volume of "invisible wastes" such as gases, particulates and fluids, becomes clearer, even though the tonnage of processed resource in use or in stock at any one time is probably impossible to calculate. Atmospheric pollution, a prominent "invisible" waste, has been measured and analyzed in some localities. Table 2 gives the results for a large urban center.

National figures for airborne particulates, gases, and aerosols cannot be calculated with accuracy although it has been estimated that manufacturing industry is responsible for about 140,000 tons of particulates every year. On the assumption that the New York breakdown approximates to all Northern urban areas and that the emissions from Southern and Western cities are lower, a total weight of about 2 million tons seems probable. By contrast one major volcanic eruption can project 20 million tons of particles into the atmosphere, much of it rising above rain scrubbing action and thus remaining in suspension for months or years. Most man-made atmospheric pollutants do not rise this high and seldom project their effects further than thirty miles from their source.

The tonnage of "invisible" waste dispersed into water is probably greater than that dissipated by air, but it is equally difficult to measure accurately. The generation of electricity and the production of major metals require no less than 125 billion tons of cooling water annually whereas municipal refuse is waterborne and water-dispersed after treatment in sewage plants. Perhaps as much as 1 billion tons of solid material vanishes in the form of heat, particulate, or fluid waste into water.

Taken together, these figures suggest that about 75 percent of the 6 billion tons of fuel and raw materials fed annually into the U.S. economy can be traced to tangible products, foodstuffs, wastes, or pollutions; the remaining 1.5 billion tons vanishes in the form of heat or gas.

Source: McCormac, 1971

Table 2. **Sources of Airborne Particulates in New York City**

Source	Tons per Year	Percentage
Space heating of apartments	20,300	32.3
Municipal incineration	12,200	19.3
Apartment incineration	11,600	18.4
Mobile sources	9,000	14.3
Electric power generation	5,800	9.2
Industry	4,100	6.5
Total	63,000	

The Mining Industry

As Table 3 shows, world production of minerals has increased rapidly since World War II, and the declining quality of ores has so far been offset by advances in extraction technology. A side effect of this trend has been the increasing quantity of ore of all types that must be processed in order to produce the same amount of metal. As we shall see in Chapter 4, the Germans were the first to gear their mining industry to the exploitation of large quantities of poor quality ore instead of small quantities of high quality ore. This technique has now been widely adopted, and, as a result, on average, forty times as much waste rock and tailings are produced per ton of metal as was the case a generation ago.

At present the continental United States is responsible for 60 percent of the world's annual production of molybdenum, 55 percent of its china clay, 41 percent of its phosphate rock, 25 percent of its copper, 19 percent of its coal, 15 percent of its lead, 12 percent of its iron ore, 10 percent of its zinc, and 4 percent of its gold. The largest waste product of this enormous mining activity is waste rock, the coarse material excavated to expose ore-bearing strata. This is closely followed by mill tailings, the residue resulting from the separation of minerals from their ores. Waste generated by the sizing and cleaning of coal, either from underground mining or strip mining, also contributes a large component as does dredging spoil (which is generally included because its mineralogi-

Table 3. World Production of Selected Minerals

Source: Down and Stocks, 1977

	Millions of Tons per Year		
Mineral	1941	1961	1973
Aluminum (bauxite)	6.0	28.5	70.0
Asbestos	0.6	2.5	5.5
China clay	2.0	7.0	16.0
Chrome ore	1.6	4.1	6.8
Coal	1,745.0	2,440.0	2,245.0
Copper metal	2.5	4.2	6.4
Fluorspar	0.4	2.0	5.0
Gypsum	12.0	41.0	60.0
Iron ores	228.0	499.0	864.0
Lead, metal in ore	1.7	2.4	3.5
Manganese ore	5.7	13.8	21.3
Nickel, metal in ore	0.15	0.37	0.68
Phosphate rock	10.1	45.0	97.0
Potash (K_2O)	3.1	9.9	19.0
Pyrites	—	17.9	22.0
Salt	37.0	83.0	150.0
Tin, metal in ore	0.24	0.16	0.24
Zinc, metal in ore	2.1	3.3	5.5

cal and physical state resembles that of other mining wastes even though it originates in agriculture). Another major waste is phosphate slime, which is pumped into large ponds for eventual settlement.

Table 4 gives the annual production and estimated accumulation already in existence of the principle mining wastes. As the figures in Table 4 show, the U.S. mining industry's annual output of 1.5 billion tons of waste rock and 0.5 billion tons of auriferous tailings contributes to a growing accumulation of mining waste estimated in 1977 to stand at 16.6 billion tons. As early as 1965 it was calculated that 14,000 square miles of land were either disturbed or covered by mining waste, and this figure — approximately equal to one-half of 1 percent of the land surface — is steadily increasing because of the working out of rich deposits and exploitation of poorer ones.

The copper industry alone is responsible for more

Source: Clifton, Brown, and Frohndorff, 1977

Table 4. Large-Scale U.S. Mining Wastes

Mining Industry	Millions of Tons per Year		
	Waste Rock	Tailings	Accumulation
Copper	624	234	7,700
Dredge spoil	300	—	—
Taconite	100	109	3,600
Coal	—	100	2,700
Phosphates	230	54	907
Iron ore	27	27	730
Gold	15	5	450
Uranium	156	5.8	110
Lead	0.5	8	180
Zinc	0.9	7.2	180
Quarry	68	—	—
Gypsum	14.2	2.7	—
Asbestos	0.6	2	14
Barite	1.9	3.1	24
Fluorspar	0.1	0.4	—

than half of all mining waste, with iron ore and taconite, coal, uranium, phosphates, gold, gypsum, lead, and zinc also large contributors. The major copper-producing areas are in Arizona, Utah, Montana, Michigan, and Tennessee. Iron ore is found in Minnesota, Michigan, Missouri, Pennsylvania, California, and Wyoming, and lower-grade taconite ores are heavily mined from Minnesota's Messabi Range. Lead and zinc are still mined in Idaho, Tennessee, and Wisconsin, and abandoned mining areas such as those in Missouri, Kansas, and Oklahoma and the Mother Lode district of Northern California either retain large waste rock and tailing deposits or are being actively reworked with new machinery.

The largest deposits of coal mining waste are to be found in the Eastern states of Pennsylvania, West Virginia, Tennessee, and Kentucky, with 3 billion tons in Pennsylvania and Kentucky alone; but there are also significant deposits in Illinois, Ohio, and Wyoming. It is anticipated that the rate of production of coal mining waste will increase from 100 million tons a year at present to 250 million tons by the year 2000 as a result of increasing exploitation of coal as an energy source.

The fourth largest accumulation of mining waste after copper, taconite, and coal is generated by the phosphate fertilizer industry, which operates chiefly in Florida. There, mining takes the form of strip extraction with the creation of long trenches flanked by piles of overburden containing huge lagoons of phosphate slime up to a mile and half in width. The accumulated tonnage of phosphate slime in 1977 was estimated at nearly 2 billion, with an average water content of 75 percent. The clay particles in the slime precipitate very slowly so that even after twenty-five years, evaporation has only increased their solid content by 5 percent. Silica sand, which constitutes the other half of the waste product of the industry, is produced in smaller quantities than slime and has several marketable uses.

The figure of 4 billion tons annually was given earlier as the rate at which topsoil was lost from agricultural land by erosion, irrigation, and cultivation. This quantity of material, passing in surface water to collect in larger rivers, is not often economically retrievable. Where it is, in major navigable rivers such as the Mississippi and the Columbia, it is sucked off the bottom as dredge spoil at the rate of 300 million tons a year. Although some dredge spoil is used in landfill, the majority of it is dumped in open water.

Quarrying operations in sand and gravel pits should

also be mentioned here because fully 40 percent of the land disturbed by mining operations is traceable to this cause. The actual production of waste rock from quarrying is, however, relatively low, at 68 million tons a year.

Since only a tiny fraction of all mining waste is used for any other purpose than self-containment in mounds or lakes, it is interesting to consider the volume that will be generated in the future if currently anticipated rates of growth eventuate. Recent projections suggest that U.S. industry will consume 7 billion tons of iron ore, 1.5 billion tons of bauxite, and 1 billion tons of phosphates over the next 100 years. These mineral resources will generate a minimum of 56 billion tons of waste rock, tailings, and slimes covering nearly 20,000 square miles of land surface. Characteristically, the exhaustion of the taconite ores in the 120-mile-long Messabi Range will create a 230,000-acre lake where none existed before. Exploitation of resources of this order will require the development of undersea mining and presumably also of undersea waste disposal techniques.

Agriculture

It is curious at first sight that agriculture, concerned as it is with products that are biodegradable by definition, should be the second largest producer of waste even when topsoil loss is not included. The reason for this paradox is that intensive and traditional agriculture involve entirely different processes with different cycles of residue production and utilization. Traditional nonintensive agriculture involved the use of the land to provide fuel, fiber, shelter, and food in the form of crops and animals. A portion of the residues generated by harvesting and processing was used by the consumer, and the remainder was returned to the land as fertilizer. This method had the benefit of optimum utilization of waste but resulted in a low level of total agricultural productivity. In the present century, and especially since World War II, increasing energy consumption through mechanization and the use of inorganic fertilizers has increased agricultural productivity and decreased the real cost of food, but, as a consequence, the original link between the consumer and the land has been broken, and agricultural waste problems have grown alarmingly.

Today, intensive agriculture has made it possible for 5 million farm workers to produce quantities of food that would necessitate the work of 30 million peasant farmers, but this revolution has been achieved at the cost of a considerable increase in the average size of farms and a vast dislocation of the traditional waste-fertilization cycle. Livestock production offers a clear example, for the number of beef cattle raised in the United States has increased by 75 percent since 1945 to over 50 million head, and the resultant waste output (each 900-pound steer produces 17 pounds of urine and 40 pounds of solid waste a day) now represents a serious waste disposal problem. Runoff from beef cattle feedlots, many of which hold more than 40,000 animals, has been calculated at 200 million tons annually and contains dangerous concentrations of oxygen-consuming compounds as well as high levels of nitrogen and phosphorus, all of which lead to surface water pollution and fish kills. Large cattle feedlots generate the same kind of waste disposal problems that faced towns in the nineteenth century, when waterborne sewage systems were introduced at great cost to avert health risks that in feedlots are dealt with by antibiotics.

Food crops too have responded to intensive production by the creation of new waste disposal problems. Field wastes were traditionally plowed back into the earth where they decayed as organic enrichment for the soil, but modern cropping methods, which in the Sunbelt produce two crops a season, mean that this material must be removed from the area of cultivation before re-planting. As a result, more than half the 250,000 acres of rice stubble in California is burned every year, as is much of the grass grown for seeding lawns. Sugar cane in the

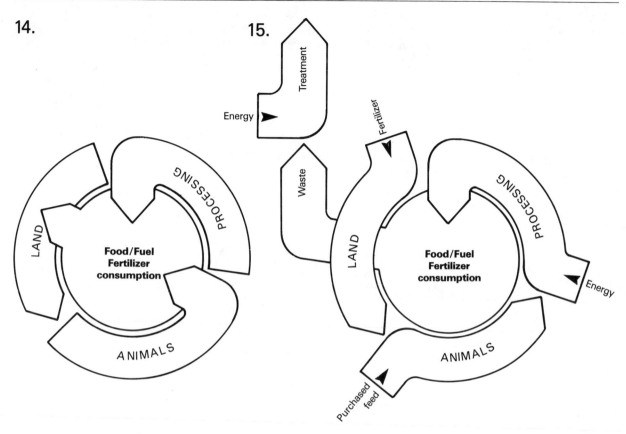

14.

15.

LAND

PROCESSING

**Food/Fuel
Fertilizer
consumption**

ANIMALS

Treatment

Energy

Fertilizer

Waste

LAND

PROCESSING

**Food/Fuel
Fertilizer
consumption**

Energy

ANIMALS

Purchased feed

14. A diagrammatic representation of the operations of the traditional agriculture. Although yields were small by modern standards, all waste products were fed back into and absorbed by the land, which was also the sole energy source.

15. Modern intensive agriculture has permitted enormously increased food yields, but at the price of external energy and nutrient inputs and the production of waste in greater quantities than the land can absorb. Disposal or neutralization of this waste requires a further energy input.

South and orchard wastes in the Northeast and Northwest are also burned in large quantities. Crop farming operations in general produce more than 150 million tons of straws, oilseed hulls, and corn cobs annually, and commercial vegetable production is responsible for another 300 million tons of organic waste. Even the smallest food cannery produces as much organic waste as a town of 15,000 people. Forestry produces 25 million tons a year of bark, wood chips, and forest sweepings and another 30 million tons of wood residues in saw mills and paper-making plants.

All the traditional methods of allowing the land to absorb wastes are overwhelmed by the quantity and frequency of these new intensive processes. Composting can be effective in appropriate locations but cannot feasibly cope with the volume and strength of many wastes. In the same way, the generation of methane gas, although valuable as a farming energy source, does nothing to reduce the bulk of the wastes employed. Cattle feedlots, if approximated to human settlements on the basis of their runoff quantity, often call for the introduction of millions of gallons of water for dilution or sewage processing where no such water supplies are available.

As a result of these growing pressures on the land, food processing wastes, feedlot runoff, and atmospheric pollution from waste burning will soon be joined by a new generation of difficulties resulting from the accumulation of nitrogen compounds introduced in fertilizer and the serious loss of agricultural land through erosion. Ultimately, inorganic materials such as salts, metals, and other residues will build up in dangerous quantities.

Underlying the increase in waste products generated by intensive agriculture is the loss of topsoil, which multiplies its effects. The 4 billion tons of particulate matter reaching the nation's waterways from this source annually is not only 700 times greater than the sum of all sewage discharges but represents the loss of hundreds of years of natural soil production brought about by weather and wild plant life. The loss of water storage capacity in reservoirs caused by silt adds up to 300 billion gallons a year whereas a bare 30 million tons of topsoil is returned to the land in the form of dredge spoil. Ever since the New Deal, dams and storage basins have been built across the country in an effort to slow this loss:

contour plowing and planting and strip cropping are also used to the same end but to little ultimate effect. Table 5 suggests an approximate breakdown for all agricultural wastes; these figures should be balanced against the 400 percent increase in farm productivity achieved since 1930.

Table 5. Agricultural Wastes in the United States by Weight

Wastes	Millions of Tons
Topsoil loss	4,000
Commercial vegetable production	300
Livestock	200
Straw, oilseed hulls, etc.	150
Saw and paper mills	30
Forest residues	25
Total	4,705

Industry

Compared with mining and agriculture, the industrial sector of the U.S. economy offers a well-developed example of adaptation in terms of waste utilization and the control or diminution of older waste accumulations. Despite the very large volumes of raw material processed by many industries, particularly those devoted to refining the products of the mining sector, the relative quantities of waste produced are small and in most cases owe more to combustion — the production of heat for processing or fabrication from fossil fuels — than any intrinsically poor utilization of the material itself. Indeed, the high value of most fabrication materials is reflected in the small losses sustained in the production process. Steel, for example, shows only a 27 percent loss from raw to refined state, and all but 3 percent of that loss constitutes revert scrap — which can be fed back into production. All such processes, however, employ large quantities of cooling water. Steel making consumes 40,000 gallons of water per finished ton, while a small (10,000 barrels a day) oil refinery will use as much water as a town of 20,000 people, and a sulphite paper mill the same quantity as a city of 500,000.

The major industrial solid wastes are the by-products of combustion or the results of incomplete chemical processing, and the control or development of uses for these residues represents a major waste disposal issue. Table 6 shows the estimated quantity of combustion or process waste generated by some major industries. These wastes occur in the form of slags, ash, dust, slimes, and gas scrubber waste. Existing accumulations of these wastes, dominated by fly ash, probably add up to 450 million tons, and their location is closely related to areas of urbanization because the largest amounts of fossil fuel are burned not in mining but in highly populated industrial zones.

About 50 million tons (1.5 percent) of the solid waste produced every year from all sources is classified as toxic and hazardous, with the vast majority of it coming from the chemical industry. The production of chemical compounds including plastics has expanded enormously in the years since World War II, with 2 billion

Table 6. Major U.S. Waste-Producing Industries

Industry	Millions of Tons
Iron and steel	57.5
Electricity generation (coal- and oil-fired)	54
Aluminum	6.5
Cement	5.9
Copper	5
Total	128.9

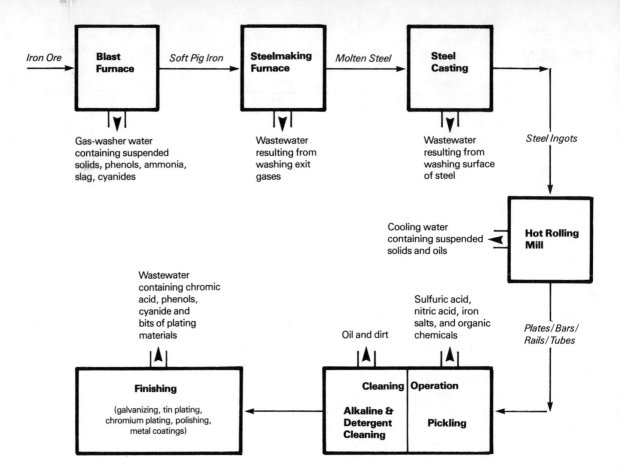

Iron Ore → **Blast Furnace** → Soft Pig Iron → **Steelmaking Furnace** → Molten Steel → **Steel Casting** → Steel Ingots

Gas-washer water containing suspended solids, phenols, ammonia, slag, cyanides

Wastewater resulting from washing exit gases

Wastewater resulting from washing surface of steel

Hot Rolling Mill

Cooling water containing suspended solids and oils

Plates/Bars/Rails/Tubes

Wastewater containing chromic acid, phenols, cyanide and bits of plating materials

Sulfuric acid, nitric acid, iron salts, and organic chemicals

Oil and dirt

Finishing
(galvanizing, tin plating, chromium plating, polishing, metal coatings)

Cleaning Operation

Alkaline & Detergent Cleaning

Pickling

16. Flow diagram for steel production, showing wastes generated at different stages. (Source: Van Tassel, 1970.)

gallons of benzene feedstock alone manufactured every year. The wastes generated by this industry have recently become notorious as a result of inadequate dumpsite protection, groundwater leaching, and the emission of toxic fumes. Though small in volume, they tend to be concentrated and complicated, requiring chemical breakdown before they can safely be dumped. The increasing tendency on the part of regulatory authorities to require this — or else perpetually guarded clay-sealed toxic landfill sites — is in the process of creating a revolution in disposal methods. The ideal circumstance, a fusion of toxic waste decomposition and biotechnology for the production of useful products, may emerge in due course.

Municipal Waste

The waste products generated by urbanization constitute the largest source of unconsumed product after mining, agriculture, and industry. At present over 180 million tons of solid waste are disposed of by municipalities every year, and the annual increase in weight is of the order of 5 percent. It is estimated that the per capita weight of municipal refuse in the United States increased from 2.7 pounds in 1920 to almost 20 pounds in 1980 whereas the density of this waste fell dramatically over the same period, indicating a great increase in volume. Table 7 shows the major components of the municipal waste stream. Studies of the large refuse element in municipal waste suggest that it can be broken down into the main constituents by weight shown in Table 8.

Sewage sludge, which constitutes 6 percent of all municipal waste by weight, is generated by the chemical treatment of municipal sewage, which is itself waterborne. The sludge is usually deposited in settling basins and allowed to thicken before being disposed of — either by waterways, incineration, or (in very limited quantities) by composting for fertilizer. Incinerator residues, just over 2 percent of all municipal waste, result from the preburning of other wastes in order to reduce their volume. In 1977 more than 150 municipal incinerators were in operation in the United States, burning 15 million tons of

Table 7. Constituents of Municipal Waste Stream

Constituents	Millions of Tons	Percentage
Refuse	135	70
Demolition waste	25	14
Sewage sludge	11	6
Glass	11	6
Incinerator residue	5	2
Rubber	5	2
Total	192	

Table 8. Constituents of Refuse

Constituents	Millions of Tons	Percentage
Paper products	50	37
Organic matter	27	20
Ash	24	18
Glass	15	11
Metals	13	10
Plastics	3	2
Unspecified	3	2
Total	135	

Source: Clifton, Brown, and Frohndorff, 1977

Source: Skitt, 1972

waste to produce only 5 million tons of residue, itself containing salvageable quantities of glass and ferrous metals.

Demolition wastes result, as the name implies, from the destruction of unwanted buildings and highways. Constituents and relative quantities vary with the age of the structure but the figures in Table 9 are typical.

With the exception of iron, steel, copper, and some wood, few demolition wastes are recycled, and most are dumped in landfill.

Glass comprises 6 percent of municipal solid waste and as much as 11 percent of household refuse, the latter generally in the form of containers. At present, bottle laws requiring the use of returnable containers are having

generated by residential and commercial areas, amounts to more than 70 percent of the solid waste stream. Its largest component is paper and paper products from packaging. Next comes organic matter in the form of food scraps and then ash from domestic and commercial incineration. The remaining components — glass, ferrous and nonferrous metals, and plastics — also derive from containers and packaging and contribute 30 percent of the weight of all domestic refuse. The container and packaging market, with an annual turnover of more than $150 billion, consumes almost as much of these critical materials as does the construction industry, and its overall recycling performance is poor. Notwithstanding voluntary industrial and municipal efforts, over 40 million tons of paper products and 6 million tons of steel in the form of cans disappear into landfill every year.

Source: Wilson, Foley, Wiesman, 1976

Table 9. Constituents of Demolition Waste

Constituents	Millions of Tons	Percentage
Concrete	18	72
Iron and steel	2.3	10
Clay products	2.2	9
Wood products	2.1	9
Aluminum	0.01	—
Copper	0.07	—
Total	25	

17. Typical constituents of household waste in their approximate proportions. (Source: Adler, 1973.)

the effect of shifting an increasing quantity of glass from household refuse to municipal landfill — a result of large-scale dumping from bottle banks, which collect many more containers than can be used as cullet by the glass industry.

Tires, which are produced at the rate of 200 million casings a year, constitute 2 percent by weight of municipal solid waste and find their way into landfill in large quantities for lack of alternative uses. Under 20 percent of all tires are recapped and returned to the highway, and even these are eventually abandoned with a serious loss of embodied energy, each casing requiring about 7.5 gallons of petroleum in its manufacture.

Municipally collected refuse, which is the waste

34

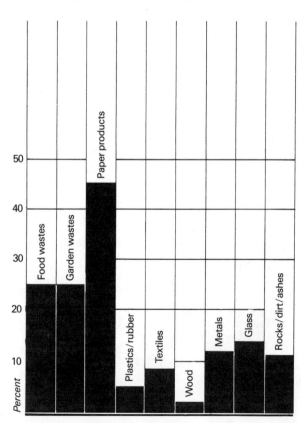

Waste Output Projections for the Future

On the basis of recent figures, the ten largest sources of waste by weight at present can be computed as in Table 10. Each of these sources is responsible for more than 100 million tons of material a year, a cutoff point that, interestingly, excludes any individual manufacturing waste except cooling or process water, which after treatment is generally returned to waterways. To attempt to project these rates of output forward for twenty years is clearly an unreliable enterprise in view of the large number of variables that can so easily intervene; nonetheless, the result is not without interest.

World demand for minerals of all kinds is expected to quadruple by the year 2000, and this estimate excludes increases in coal production for power generation, gasification, or liquefaction, as well as efforts to exploit oil shale reserves for petroleum.

Increases in agricultural output are expected to be almost as impressive, largely as a result of even more intensive land use and near-universal confined livestock production. The effects of fertilization, irrigation, multiple harvests, and the consequent wind and water erosion are expected to increase the rate of topsoil loss by as much as 30 percent, thus creating the need for remedial action on a greatly increased scale in lakes and waterways. At the same time, great increases in crop residues and animal manure output can be expected, which will in turn

Table 10. Major Waste Sources in the U.S. Economy

Source	Millons of Tons per Year	Percentage
Agriculture (topsoil)	4,000	59.8
Mining (copper)	850	12.7
Agriculture (crop residues)	390	5.8
Waterways (dredge spoil)	300	4.5
Mining (phosphates)	284	4.2
Mining (taconite)	209	3.3
Agriculture (animal manure)	200	3.1
Urbanization (municipal waste)	180	2.6
Mining (uranium)	162	2.4
Mining (coal)	100	1.4
Total	6,675	

create further problems of disposal and detoxification.

The volume of material consumed by urbanization is also expected to continue its dramatic rise, with some authorities anticipating weight increases of over 200 percent as well as proportional increases in volume. In view of the relatively high recovery value of many of the constituents of the municipal solid waste stream and the

Table 11. Major Waste Sources in the U.S. Economy, Twenty-Year Projection

Source	Millions of Tons	Percentage
Agriculture (topsoil)	5,500	32.5
Mining (copper)	3,000	17.8
Mining (oil shale)	1,500	8.9
Agriculture (crop residues)	1,400	8.3
Waterways (dredge spoil)	1,200	7.1
Mining (phosphates)	1,100	6.5
Agriculture (animal manure)	1,000	5.9
Mining (taconite)	800	4.7
Mining (uranium)	600	3.5
Mining (coal)	400	2.3
Urbanization (municipal waste)	400	2.3
Total	16,900	

current development of mechanized processing facilities, this source more than any other is extremely difficult to predict. There can be little doubt that the volume of organic wastes will increase at a slightly faster rate than the population, as it has since World War II, but the role of containers and packaging may be dramatically altered by legislation and raw material or energy shortages.

Making a pessimistic assessment of the likely success of voluntary and legislative controls over the solid waste stream and accepting recent predictions for agriculture, mining, and industry — which embody some allowance for the development of submarine mining without land-based waste implications — the picture in Table 11 of high-volume waste sources in the year 2000 may emerge. There are several remarkable things about this projected ranking of the top ten waste sources at the turn of the century. The first, of course, is that it is highly speculative, being subject to change at the hands of international and national politics, economics, technical development, and (perhaps most of all) energy availability. Furthermore, it has been compiled without reference to a whole range of synergetic effects, for example, the vast increase in effluent purification by-products that would result from the increased burning of fossil fuels or the increase in demolition wastes that would result from land use conflicts between mining and urbanization. On the other hand, the fact that these figures are compiled from government and commercial sources shows that they represent a responsible assessment of demand, if not a reliable estimate of consequent waste production. It is instructive, for instance, that the municipal waste stream, despite a projected increase in volume of over 100 percent, drops three places in Table 11 to finish last. Conversely, topsoil loss, increasing by only 37 percent, maintains its place at the head of the list whereas coal, up by 300 percent, still rises only one place.

What is really taking place, if this prediction is to be believed, is a movement in which waste output will not only rise but coalesce so that the difference in this sense between the various sectors of the economy will diminish along with their productivity. Eventually, the burden of waste required to be moved in order to extract, process, distribute, and dispose of each ton of resource will rise to a figure impossible to reconcile with predictable energy availability. In resource extraction terms, this is close to the concept of entropy in physics: that state of affairs where all thermodynamic gradients are flattened, and heat cannot profitably be directed from one substance to another.

If within twenty years the ten largest sources of waste in the U.S. economy produce 17 billion tons annually, then the total waste output from all sources will almost certainly reach 19 billion tons, and the required input of fuels and raw materials will climb from 6 billion to 15 billion tons. *That these figures are impossible does not mean that they are untrue. It is a measure of the enormous change that must come over the American economy that its present operations are predicated on rates of consumption and production that cannot feasibly be sustained for even another twenty years.*

Short of an implausibly dramatic energy breakthrough, only a radical redefinition of waste can change the disastrous implication of these figures. If only 10 percent of what is now classified as waste could be converted into a resource, a balance between raw material input and waste output could be achieved. If, by a massive scientific, technical, and conceptual effort, 50 percent could be so transformed, then the catastrophic waste output presently predicted to be realized in twenty years would not arrive for another fifty.

In order to examine the feasibility of such drastic alterations in the fate of American prosperity, it is necessary to look more closely at the nature of waste and the manner in which it has in the past been converted into a resource. This task will be undertaken in the next two chapters.

Notes

1. Owing to the large number of sources consulted in the preparation of this chapter, one section of the bibliography has been devoted to the task. Where tables are attributed, full citations can be found in this section. Where tables are unattributed, they are composite assemblages, for which the author alone accepts responsibility although the sources used in compiling them are as given in the bibliography.

3 | On the Nature of Waste

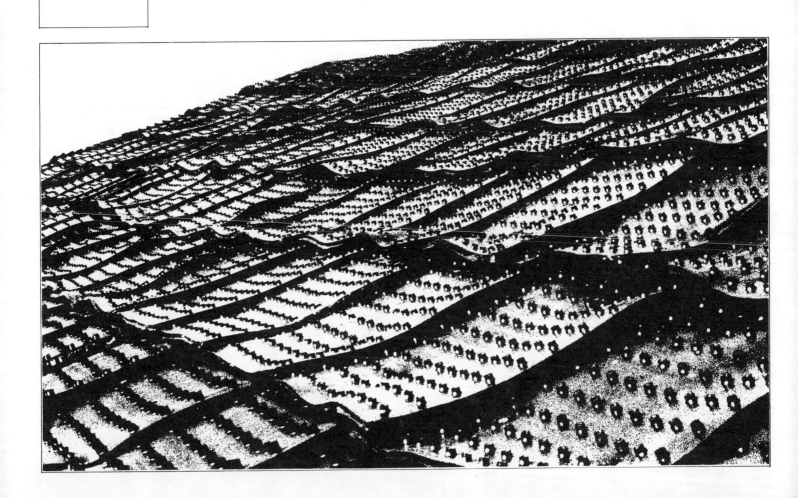

" To those who know scrap, to those who handle it and to whom it is their life, it is not prosaic nor is it to be derided. To them, scrap is something alive, as fascinating as gold dust sifting through his fingers was to the Forty-Niner. It is a vital raw material which, by the alchemy of the scrap yard will be transmuted into a brighter tomorrow. **"**

Edwin C. Barringer, *The Story of Scrap,* 1945

On the Nature of Waste

Because matter is indestructible, what we conceive to be the creation of waste is in reality the incomplete transformation of matter. Consequently, all talk of the exhaustion of resources, however alarming, is imprecise: what we really mean is the conversion of useful raw materials into useless or inaccessible ones by the operations of the economy. This definition of the workings of industrial civilization is, however, subject to some qualification; every day new resources or new ways to use what was previously thought to be useless come to light, and these new discoveries offset the steady increase in the proportion of waste relative to unused resources that the remainder of industry and urbanization brings about. At different historical periods, different balances between these two tendencies can be observed: two hundred years ago the North American Indians had a small range of resources but a very high level of resource utilization; today the North American consumer has an immense range of resources but a much lower level of resource utilization. The emphasis changes continually, like a currency exchange rate, and is only good for the time and place of the transaction.

Because of uncertainties like these, even popular definitions of waste are not simple. Thorndike and Barnhart's high school dictionary takes twenty-one lines to explain "waste" but only four to explain "computer"; and the Concise Oxford Dictionary dismisses "computer" in two lines and gives "waste" thirty-seven. These definitions, of course, include the use of the word as a verb, an adjective, and a noun, but even in the last category there are four basic meanings, none of which can be ignored in the pursuit of a true definition. They are "useless or worthless material," "bare or wild land," "wearing down little by little," and "failure to get value from." All except the first of these are generally left out of legal and technical definitions where shades of meaning are less important than lists of acknowledged waste problems. The preamble to the Federal Resource Conservation and Recovery Act of 1976 is a good example of the latter approach.

Waste means all garbage, refuse, sludge from a waste treatment plant, water supply treatment plant or air pollution control facility, and other discarded material including solid, liquid, semi-solid or contained gaseous material resulting from industrial, commercial, mining and agricultural operations, and from community activities.

To bring thermodynamic, popular, and legal definitions of waste into line requires a massive enlargement of our idea of what is and what is not waste. Beer and beverage containers at the roadside, slag heaps near coal mines, buried drums of chemicals, noxious fumes, particulate matter in air and water, junked cars, animal feedlot runoff, discarded newspapers and magazines—all of these are wastes in advanced consumer societies, but the list neither starts nor ends with man-made products. In recent years scientists have devoted a great deal of attention to apportioning the output of waste in the world between human and natural sources, and the results are surprising. Notwithstanding the massive development of industry over the last century — virtually all of it based on the burning of fossil fuels — world emissions of sulfur compounds are still predominantly natural in origin. Nearly twice as much hydrogen sulphide is given off by bacteria as sulfur dioxide by combustion. Even the sulfur dioxide given off by gasoline and diesel engines amounts to only one-third of that projected into the air by sea spray. The same is true of nitrogen compounds, more than 90 percent of which are pumped into the air by bacteria.[1]

The millions of tons of volcanic ash propelled into the atmosphere by Mount St. Helens can also be classified as waste not only because they are useless as a resource but because in geological terms they were "made poor use of" by the earth — the involuntary escape of subsurface material from the earth's core being in this sense similar to an oil spill or the plume of contaminated ground water emanating from the Niagara Love Canal. If Mount St. Helens and the Hooker Chemical Company appear equally indifferent to the havoc they cause, it is because the geological processes of the earth and the "invisible hand" of the marketplace are in this sense very similar in their operations.

In the natural world, surplus and waste are indistinguishable because interconnecting life systems ensure that the output of one process acts as the input to another. Even within the industrial economies of developed countries, where waste and surplus appear to be clearly differentiated, their interchangeability is much more obvious than we would think. Surplus grain can either be burned, in which case it is waste, or sold overseas, in which case it is a raw material for food supply. Unsold books can be stored, in which case they are a surplus, or pulped, in which case they again become a raw material. Like political prisoners who become presidents, wastes that become valuable resources are facts of human history.

Take, for example, the cannonballs cast for the Civil War more than a century ago. Large numbers of these were sold as scrap after the conflict and broken up by the old method of pouring water into their handling holes and waiting for the winter frost to crack them into fragments. These fragments in turn were fed into furnaces to make steel and rolled into rails for the nation's expanding railroad network. After up to fifty years of such service the worn-out rails were again sold as scrap, hundreds of tons of them being shipped to Europe for use as tank barriers before World War II. With the German occupation of the Continent, these tank traps were cut off at ground level with acetylene torches and shipped to German steel mills for the rolling and casting of alloy steel tank hulls and turrets; then they made their way into Russia with the invading German armies. By the end of

18. The production of solid waste by transport animals prior to the development of the gasoline engine, a classic example of the negation by progress of a hypothetical environmental threat. (Source: Adler, 1973.)

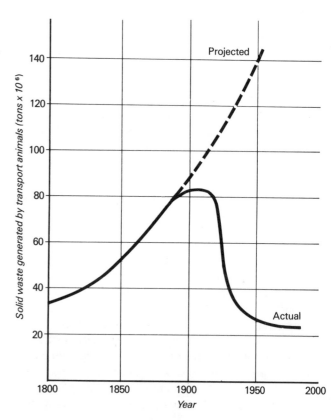

42

the war virtually all of this steel had been absorbed again by the Russia steel industry to be formed into beams, girders, truck frames, and yet more tanks—some of which found their way eventually to the Middle East, ending up in Israel after the Arab wars.

It is this unpredictable potential for resurrection that dogs all static definitions of waste. To be sure, primary recycling is not generally as well established as it is in the iron and steel industry, but there are many other examples of such chains of use and disuse. Not surprisingly more than half the gold mined thoughout history is still in circulation in one form or another, but even metals of lesser value are retrieved in considerable quantities. Over half the copper and lead used in the United States every year is scrapped and used again, as is 25 percent of the aluminum and 15 percent of the zinc. The potential for transformation and reuse exists in all wastes, at least in theory, and the manner in which this dormant potential has been trapped in the past is so little short of miraculous that only a rash or ill-informed observer would pronounce it impossible for any material at some time in the future.

The Alchemy of Waste Transformation

One case where the imposition of legislation brought about just such a reversal was that of the Leblanc process, a common means of manufacturing sodium carbonate for soap and glass 120 years ago. Initially, this system involved the roasting of sodium sulphate and limestone, which produced noxious fumes containing hydrochloric acid gas. In due course these fumes dissolved in the dew on nearby meadow grass and poisoned the cows that grazed on it. As a result, a law was passed banning the discharge of hydrochloric acid gas, and the sodium carbonate industry was forced into recession for a number of years. During this time, efforts were made to extract the gas from the effluent before discharge, eventually with such success that the Leblanc process rose to prominence again — only this time hydrochloric acid (used for bleaching textiles) was the principal product and sodium carbonate merely a subsidiary.

About thirty years after the prohibition of hydrochloric acid gas effluent a similar transformation took place in the infant petroleum industry. Ever since the first great Pennsylvania oil strike of 1859, which initiated the production of oil in volume, the principal oil product had been the lamp fuel kerosene. Of the three main fractions into which crude oil was then distilled, this was the middle or medium in terms of density. Gasoline, the chief product of the light or naptha fraction, was virtually worthless and also highly flammable, so much so that it was often burned off in pits as a hazardous waste. The heavy fraction, producing lubricating oils, waxes, and "petroleum coke," was repeatedly distilled under pressure to make it produce remnants of kerosene instead.

This market balance was disturbed in 1885 by the introduction of the incandescent gas mantle. Gas companies offered free installation and cheap gas stoves for cooking, and the bottom dropped out of the kerosene business wherever gas companies were in competition. Within a few years the oil companies faced a major recession, which was only averted by the sudden emergence of a new market for the formerly despised light fraction, gasoline. The internal combustion engine and the automobile soon created an enormous demand that dwarfed any previous records set by kerosene. Now it was the turn of the medium fraction to be repeatedly cracked until it gave up its last remnants of motor fuel and for its specific gravity to be lowered by the addition of lead so that what was once light-illuminating oil could now be sold as heavy gasoline.

The transformation of gasoline from hazardous waste to crucial resource is probably the most spectacular in the whole history of resource recovery, but it has a sequel, perhaps two sequels, both of which indicate again that *nothing* can be permanently classified as a waste. The lead tetra-ethyl added to the medium fraction

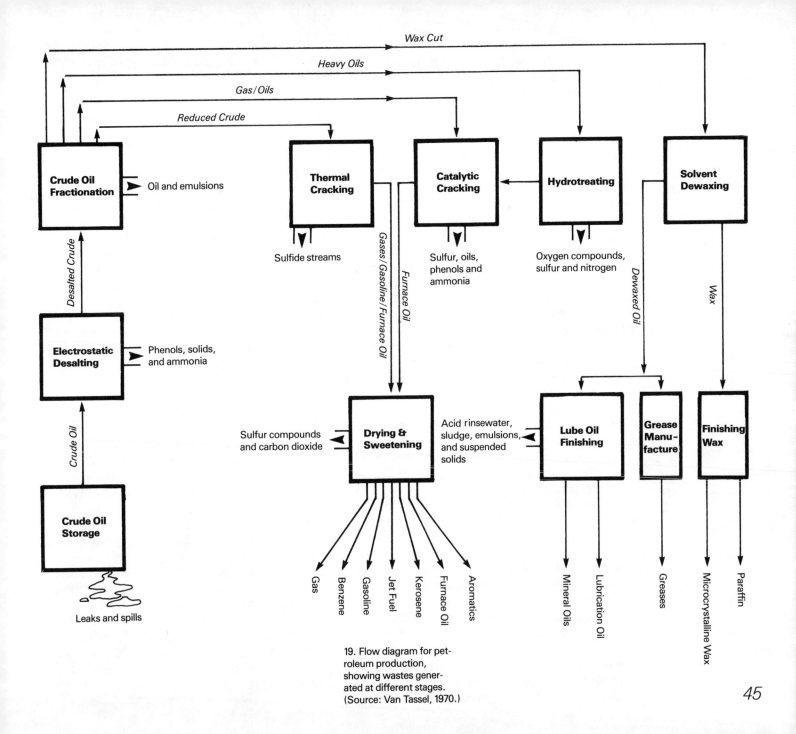

Wax Cut

Heavy Oils

Gas/Oils

Reduced Crude

Crude Oil Fractionation — Oil and emulsions

Thermal Cracking

Catalytic Cracking

Hydrotreating

Solvent Dewaxing

Sulfide streams

Sulfur, oils, phenols and ammonia

Oxygen compounds, sulfur and nitrogen

Desalted Crude

Electrostatic Desalting — Phenols, solids, and ammonia

Gases/Gasoline/Furnace Oil

Furnace Oil

Dewaxed Oil

Wax

Crude Oil

Sulfur compounds and carbon dioxide — **Drying & Sweetening**

Acid rinsewater, sludge, emulsions, and suspended solids — **Lube Oil Finishing**

Grease Manu-facture

Finishing Wax

Crude Oil Storage

Leaks and spills

Gas Benzene Gasoline Jet Fuel Kerosene Furnace Oil Aromatics

Mineral Oils Lubrication Oil

Greases

Microcrystalline Wax Paraffin

19. Flow diagram for petroleum production, showing wastes generated at different stages. (Source: Van Tassel, 1970.)

45

distillate proved eventually to have advantages for all gasoline. It enabled engines to operate at higher compression ratios without pre-ignition — the audible explosion of the last part of the fuel charge familiar to Americans who drove the first generation of unleaded gasoline cars. Since the efficiency of the gasoline engine is more or less dependent on its compression ratio, lead was used in gasoline for many years even though more than 60 percent of it was known to emerge in particle form from the vehicle's exhaust. The resultant air pollution, insignificant in 1925 when the 17 million motor vehicles on America's roads constituted more than half of all the cars in the world, became increasingly serious as the motor population increased. By 1970, when the United States boasted 100 million motor vehicles, up to 90 percent of all the atmospheric lead in urban areas could be attributed to the additive. In due course emission-control legislation led to the introduction of unleaded gasoline. Unfortunately, within a very short time it became evident that the new fuel was having a negative effect on the overall efficiency of motor transport. Legislative action in favor of air quality turned out to be a poor compromise with energy conservation, for in terms of engine efficiency, the lead additive more than paid its way. Every ton of lead added to gasoline saved the equivalent of 125 tons of fuel by ensuring better burning and higher temperature operation whereas the net saving in lead production achieved by unleaded amounted to the equivalent of only 5 tons of gasoline.

Here is a clear example of the weakness of the static rather than the dynamic definition of waste. It may be that unleaded gasoline is a good compromise between the motor vehicle and air pollution, but the energy penalty cannot be ignored. Improved efficiency may not justify the release of lead into the atmosphere, but a deeper understanding of the overall waste equation might have produced a different answer than unleaded gasoline. The example of the Leblanc process might have indicated some method of trapping the lead at emission stage and thereafter developing some use or reuse for it. That such a solution is not purely theoretical is strongly suggested by a recent European Economic Community study,[2] which recommended the introduction of muffler filters capable of intercepting more than 50 percent of the lead emitted by regular gasoline without affecting the performance of the engine — saving equivalent to 75 percent of the lead unconsumed by combustion.

The second sequel to the conversion of gasoline from waste to vital fuel involves another by-product, sulfur. Part of the struggle to develop petroleum as an energy source involved the removal of sulfur from crude oil. Many of the Western Hemisphere's richest oil reserves were heavily laden with sulfur, which rendered them unusable for illumination, then, as we have seen, the principal market. The invention of the Frasch process solved this problem by 1890, and vast reserves of so-called "Lima crude" became available; but under this system the sulfur was extracted by combining it with metal oxides in a precipitate, and it then had to be burned off in order to reuse the oxides. Like hydrochloric acid gas in the Leblanc process, the resultant fumes were a serious air pollutant; so, as the oil industry expanded in the era of the automobile, the sulfur fumes were made to yield elemental sulfur, which became a by-product of the refining process. With the passage of time, the quantity of sulfur produced by refineries, allied to that extracted by gas scrubbers from the flues of other fossil fuel industries, began to rival that of the sulfur-mining industry. In 1970 the balance was calculated at 12 million tons worldwide from flue extraction versus 16 million tons produced by mining. So badly has the development of markets for sulfur lagged behind its voluntary and involuntary rate of production that millions of tons of it have been stockpiled or dumped in the sea. In Canada huge mountains of sulfur have already accumulated against the day when some use will emerge, and at last it appears possible that it has. The product is a form of concrete using sulfur instead of Portland cement, which consumes only 10 percent of the energy needed to make conventional concrete, and its potential uses in engineering and construction are so many and varied that sulfur may one day become as important a product of petroleum as gasoline itself.

The examples of the Leblanc process, unleaded

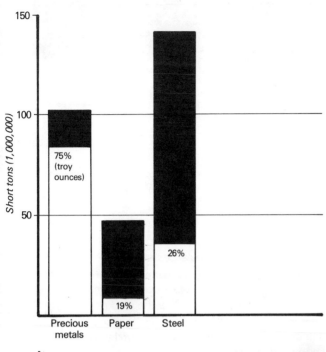

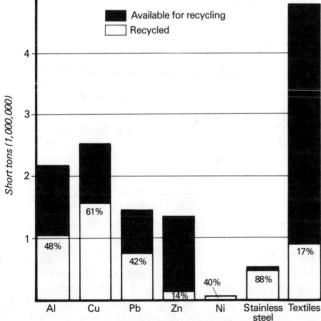

gasoline, and sulfur are important in considering the real meaning of waste in an industrial economy. Technology continually forces a bridge between waste and resource if only because the search for adequate supplies of raw materials becomes increasingly difficult. Advanced machinery now makes it economical to reprocess copper wastes left by the mining operations of fifty years ago in order to extract ores that could not be reached at that time. In the same way, coal recovery from slag heaps by washing and the mining of fluorspar from old lead mine wastes are now established processes.

Generalizing from all these developments, one can argue that the problem of waste is slowly being removed by improvements in transformation technologies. It is precisely this argument that is put forward by proponents of nuclear energy when they claim that nuclear wastes suitable for reprocessing are a resource rather than a waste, even though the reprocessing and disposal technologies are not yet perfected. The difficulty here lies in the unpredictable rate of progress over the whole spectrum of wastes of the chains of use and reuse, which are, in isolated instances, highly successful. Given an infinite period of time to perfect an overall waste consumption system, there is little doubt that the performance of iron and steel, chemicals, and petroleum could be repeated in virtually all sectors. Towns and cities could be built in the vicinity of strip mines to absorb their waste rock and tailings as concrete aggregate and landfill, and crop residues and manure could be pyrolysed to produce gas to power agricultural machinery. The difficulty is that market forces do not automatically take this direction. In some sectors of the economy these are profitable goals; in others, they can only be contemplated as the outcome of massive public expenditure.

20. Recoverable material resources currently recycled and available for recycling. (Source: Bond and Straub, 1973.)

The Evolutionary Perspective

In many ways the essence of the problem of waste is contained in this apparent conflict between economic forces and evolutionary needs. Clearly, the motive power behind the development of waste recovery technologies in iron and steel, chemicals, and petroleum is economic. Equally clearly, the theory that all waste tends toward an ultimate utility is an evolutionary idea, for it is in the natural world that the models for chains of use and reuse are found, and here the principle is bent to the service of the evolutionary goal of species survival. In nature, accumulations of waste create evolutionary opportunities precisely because they are indistinguishable from accumulations of surplus; in industrial economies accumulations of waste do not immediately create economic opportunities and cannot always be defined as surplus in any economic sense.

In part, of course, this contradiction is the result of a technical incapacity that still constitutes a serious stumbling block to resource recovery in many sectors of the economy. We do not yet know *how* to stem the loss of 4 billion tons of topsoil every year any more than we know how to store nuclear or toxic wastes for hundreds of years without risk. But an integral part of this technical limitation is our failure to emulate the larger relationship with the environment, which is the key to evolutionary opportunity in the natural world.

The massive accumulations of waste in our society result from a drastic imbalance between the power of products and the power of the environment into which they are propelled by the operations of the economy. This imbalance applies whether the product itself is a waste or merely a volume product that becomes waste. Either way, the short-run economics of the producing industry defy the basic rule of evolution — the absolute power of the environment to extinguish the species if it fails to conform to the rules of survival. The very urgency of the pollution problem in the modern world is proof of the futility of this defiance, for fears of the collapse of industrial societies through uncontrolled waste merely confirm the final power of the environment over all species, including man.

When environmentalists talk about the need to restore a balance with nature, they ignore the inconvenient fact that balance *will* ultimately be restored by the kind of collapse predicted a decade ago by the MIT *Limits of Growth* report.[3] Instead, they ask for something much more difficult, the achievement of a balance with nature in which man retains his privileged position above evolution — in effect, the control of the environment by a species. To state that this is the real goal of many environmentalists places their efforts, and their chances of success, in the correct perspective. There can be no victory over the demands of the environment, nor can there even be a negotiated peace without prior accept-

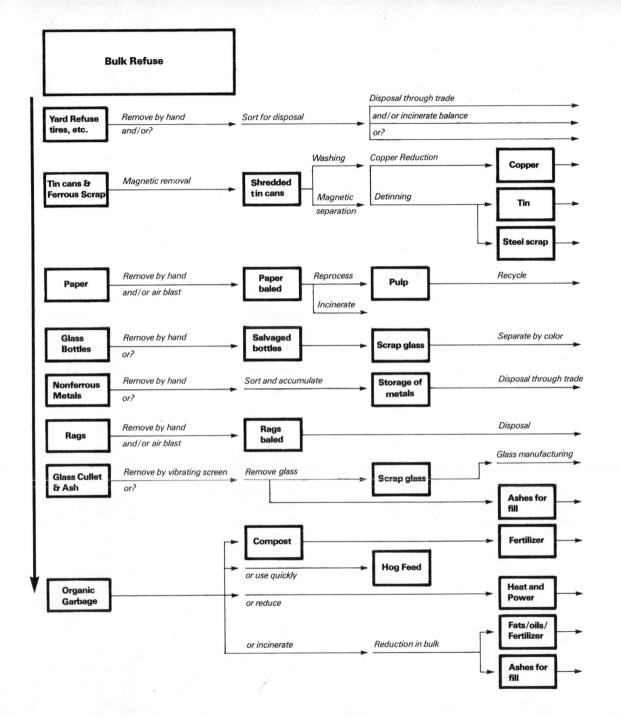

Bulk Refuse

Yard Refuse tires, etc. → *Remove by hand and/or?* → *Sort for disposal* → *Disposal through trade* / *and/or incinerate balance* / *or?*

Tin cans & Ferrous Scrap → *Magnetic removal* → **Shredded tin cans** → *Washing* → *Copper Reduction* → **Copper** ; *Magnetic separation* → *Detinning* → **Tin** , **Steel scrap**

Paper → *Remove by hand and/or air blast* → **Paper baled** → *Reprocess* → **Pulp** → *Recycle* ; *Incinerate*

Glass Bottles → *Remove by hand or?* → **Salvaged bottles** → **Scrap glass** → *Separate by color*

Nonferrous Metals → *Remove by hand or?* → *Sort and accumulate* → **Storage of metals** → *Disposal through trade*

Rags → *Remove by hand and/or air blast* → **Rags baled** → *Disposal*

Glass Cullet & Ash → *Remove by vibrating screen or?* → *Remove glass* → **Scrap glass** → *Glass manufacturing* ; **Ashes for fill**

Organic Garbage → **Compost** → **Fertilizer** ; *or use quickly* → **Hog Feed** ; *or reduce* → **Heat and Power** ; *or incinerate* → *Reduction in bulk* → **Fats/oils/Fertilizer** , **Ashes for fill**

21. Flow diagram of typical complexities in the municipal waste-processing industry, resulting from the incompatibility and non-degradability of wastes, suggests the drastic imbalance between the power of the product and the power of the environment. (Source: Bond and Straub, 1973.)

49

ance of its ultimate control. *When we think we are destroying the environment, we are in fact inviting it to destroy us as a species, which it can undoubtedly do.*

Acceptance of the power of the environment means the abandonment of one state of consciousness in favor of another. In terms of waste and pollution the price of accepting species defeat must be the movement of the economics of production and consumption onto a new time scale where transformations of material can be carried on for centuries without ruinous accumulations of waste.

Just as waste and surplus blur and merge with the adoption of an overall perspective, so with the perspective of evolutionary time does the difference between man-made and natural products lose its importance. All our products, from raw materials to razor blades, can be seen as variations that are manufactured by the species man — *extensions* of man in the sense that Marshall McLuhan applied the phrase to media. Their period of use varies, from nonexistence in the case of an industrial waste or the heat radiated uselessly from an automobile muffler, to ten years or more in the case of the automobile itself, perhaps eighty years for a house, conceivably a thousand for the cast-iron dome of the Capitol in Washington, D.C. Ultimately, all products reveal themselves to be temporarily stable configurations in a continuous transformation of matter. When their use is ended, their transformation resumes, and they are either recycled or returned to the natural environment. It is at this point that we define some of them as waste and, by measuring their quantity and toxicity, determine the threat they hold for the future of our own species. There

is a certain illogicality here that reflects the gap presently separating economic and evolutionary thinking. From the standpoint of evolution, a car in use on the Los Angeles freeway system constitutes a greater threat to the survival of the species than does an auto hulk in a junk yard. From the standpoint of the economy, use represents the opposite to waste, and no vehicle actually in motion can be of negative value. The conflict is fundamental but by no means wholly negative since only a synthesis of value in use and the needs of survival can help humanity now.

This paradox can be seen clearly if we adopt a new definition of waste that embodies some evolutionary insight, calling it, for example, "that which, *at a given time,* is produced but not consumed." This terminology incorporates waste and product-in-use into a single category and still retains the implication that matters can be changed if new uses are found and new consumption results — as it did in our earlier examples: hydrochloric acid gas, gasoline, and sulfur. The key difference between such a definition and its predecessors cited at the beginning of this chapter is contained in the phrase "at a given time" because it admits the time dimension that renders the waste problem amenable to solution. The status of product in use is preferable to that of waste in economic terms, obviously so; if it were not, there would be no distinction between an $80 billion missile system and a few thousand dollars worth of scrap metal and electrical parts. The problem is to translate this economic value into an evolutionary value, and *this can only be done by treating use as a form of resource storage over time,* so that all products retain their value as resources in the same way that natural species and organisms do.

Models from Nature

A striking example of the concept of use as storage occurred during the gas famine of 1974 when it was pointed out by some commentators that the 100 million motor vehicles in the United States — assuming each had 5 gallons of gasoline in its fuel tank — constituted a reserve of 500 million gallons. In the same sense it might have been argued that the vehicles themselves embodied a reserve of 200 million tons of steel, that 80 million houses represented forty years of building materials, or that 8 million supermarkets represented six weeks emergency rations. Such facts are obvious when they are pointed out, but the "reserves" in question are not conceived in this way. In the natural world a plant or animal represents a temporary assembly of elements negotiable in the carbon cycle; in addition to its own life, it is the embodiment of other lives and other evolutionary possibilities that will be accessed as soon as it dies. So great are the similarities between our products and the species and organisms that crowd the natural environment that it should not be impossible to design a system of uses that would, in an economic sense, reenact this drama of natural integration.

Consider the products of the consumer sector, all of which from Mercedes cars to book matches sooner or later become waste. Like natural organisms, such products are assemblages of matter set free in the world for variable periods and then terminated by functional failure or destruction. Both industrial products and natural organisms evolve and adapt according to the rigors of the environment in which they find themselves. The mechanism by which an automated drawing and ironing machine in a canning plant turns out 1,200 beverage cans every minute is actually very similar to that which enables a tree to produce an enormous superfluity of seeds or a frog an immensely redundant number of eggs. In fact, the actual rate of recycling achieved with the aid of bottle laws is very close to the survival rate achieved by frog eggs and considerably better than the reproduction rate of trees. *There is nothing "unnatural" about massive overproduction, but the containers produced by nature — the nut shell, the seed pod, the rice hull — can be produced indefinitely from resources organized cyclically for the purpose. Man-made containers of steel, aluminum, plastic, or glass could not even be maintained in production at current rates for a century for fear of resource exhaustion.*

The difference lies in the power of the environment over the abortive product in each case. Waste nut shells, seed pods, and rice hulls are very rapidly absorbed into the natural ecosystem through decomposition. Bottles or metal cans that are not retrieved for recycling remain in the natural environment, do not decompose rapidly, and

51

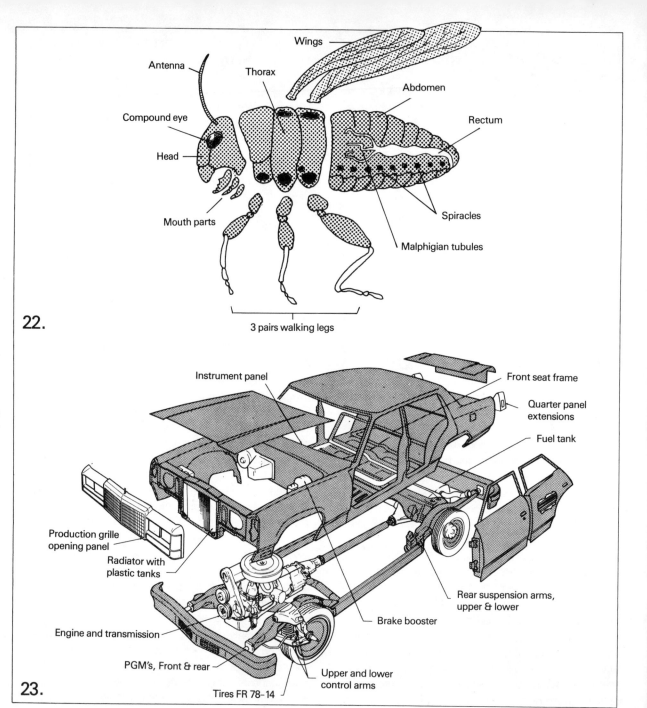

22 and 23. As these two drawings show, the characteristics of products and organisms can be made to appear very similar, and the same evolutionary analysis can be applied to both. The important thing is to emulate in the product world the sophisticated metamorphic and self-disposal capability of the organism.

22.

Wings

Antenna

Thorax

Abdomen

Compound eye

Rectum

Head

Spiracles

Mouth parts

Malphigian tubules

3 pairs walking legs

23.

Instrument panel

Front seat frame

Quarter panel extensions

Fuel tank

Production grille opening panel

Radiator with plastic tanks

Engine and transmission

Rear suspension arms, upper & lower

Brake booster

PGM's, Front & rear

Upper and lower control arms

Tires FR 78-14

are too widely dispersed for economical recovery. Thus, their role as "storage" for aluminum, steel, and glass is extremely poorly played.

A student of the evolution of waste looking at this whole issue might conclude that while the continued production of nonreturn, nonrecyclable, nonreusable, and nonbiodegradable containers must cease, a return to the returnable containers of a generation ago is a hopelessly obsolete way of bringing this about. He might further conclude that mining the solid waste stream with costly automated machinery scarcely represents an alternative at the present state of the art and with regard to the quantity of waste containers that would, for the foreseeable future, remain out of range of such facilities. The real problem lies within the container industry itself and the poor level of product evolution reached by its standard "species," not because these products are unsophisticated from the point of view of the manufacturer — the aluminum or tin-free steel can is in ways a masterpiece of advanced production technology — but because they have evolved without reference to their economic destination. A good parallel would be with the total-loss lubrication system used in the earliest gasoline engines; it did not take very long before the steady dumping of oil on the highway by cars led to the development of recirculating lubrication by an engine-driven oil pump. What has happened in the container industry has been exactly the reverse — a recirculating system gave place to a total loss process, which is now rather inefficiently being converted back by recycling. Looked at in terms of natural cycles, this seems laborious compared with what might be done with the nonreturn container.

In dealing with waste, we are exploring a subject as variable and ubiquitous as a whole range of natural species even though we treat it as one. Between them, recycling and resource recovery comprise a wide variety of techniques, but not compared with the bewildering variety of strategies for survival adopted within and between species in nature. Wastes whose retrieval requires periodic outbursts of legal activity based on media scare stories are hardly successful species; nor does the present framework of litter laws, mandatory deposit rules, recycling programs, hazardous waste regulations, and smog alerts adequately reproduce the rigor of the natural environment in dealing with delinquent organisms. In nature, regulation is built in through an automated system of decomposition and renewal; in the man-made world it is fragmentary, inefficient, and unimaginative.

What is most noticeable about our waste product species is the almost complete absence of the complex supportive and exploitive interfaces between species in nature. Although there are exceptions within major industries such as iron and steel, petroleum and chemicals, our most valuable wastes in general are conceived and disposed of without thought for the possibilities that might emerge from attempts to emulate commensalism, mutualism, or parasitism in the natural world. There are already isolated examples of how this might be done; in the emerging field of biotechnology, treated sewage can be made to yield proteins and fats, and bacteria can leach out coal from slag heaps. In theory, any such process occurring in nature can be artificially re-created.

All of these possibilities exist, but their implementation remains undercapitalized and unrelated to a general strategy of waste and energy interaction. The absence of uniform chains of production, consumption, and decomposition; the negligible incidence of energy- and resource-saving connections between industries and across product lines; the confining of product lives to a single use without metamorphic potential — all add up to an indictment of our whole conception of what waste is. Under present conditions the species controls the environment instead of the other way about — and that is why we are unable to transform waste into a resource even though we know it holds this potential.

Short-life products are no more unnatural than short-life insects or fish, and none need be wasteful in an evolutionary sense — provided they are resource carriers and not resource dissipators. The "wastefulness" of consumer societies is a function of their unbalanced efficiency, which enables them to produce but not to *reproduce* without extraordinary pressures upon them.

As environmentalists have long understood, the

best examples of ingenuity and efficiency in the elimination of waste are to be found in countries poorer than the United States, where plenty obscures the need for change. Unfortunately, anthropological zeal has generally led this search for good examples into bizarre comparisons between twentieth-century American consumers and preindustrial Indian tribes. A far more valuable direction exists in the fate of Germany in the first half of the present century when a combination of highly advanced science and technology with crippling raw material shortages under siege conditions brought about evolutionary changes in production, consumption, and reproduction that have important lessons for the energy- and resource-starved America of the future.

Notes

1. These generalizations are based on estimates made in B. M. McCormac, ed., *Introduction to the Scientific Study of Atmospheric Pollution* (Amsterdam: Reidel, 1971). Theodore B. Taylor and Charles C. Humpstone give pessimistic projections for the reversal of this balance by the year 2000 in *The Restoration of the Earth* (New York: Harper & Row, 1973).
2. Frank Ireland, ed., *The Cost of Coping with Lead in Petrol* (London: Fellowship of Engineering, 1980). Since the publication of this report Associated Octel has announced the development of a muffler filter capable of recapturing lead when it emerges as metallic particles in vehicle exhaust fumes. The filter will last for 60,000 miles and cut lead emissions by 90 percent in urban driving and 60 percent on the highway. The cost of the filter is estimated at $60.00.
3. D. H. Meadows, D. L. Meadows, J. Randers, and W. E. Behrens, *The Limits of Growth* (New York: Universe, 1972). Although the projections contained in this report have been attacked on the basis that material substitutions were not factored in, the *ultimate* implications of continued growth are clearly in this direction.

Germany: The Forgotten Miracle

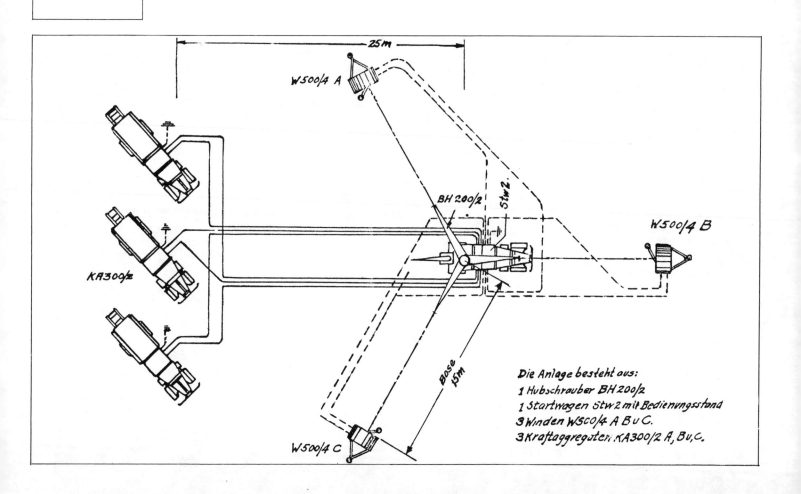

25 m

W500/4 A

BH 200/2

Stw 2.

W500/4 B

KA300/2

Base 15m

W500/4 C

Die Anlage besteht aus:
1 Hubschrauber BH 200/2
1 Startwagen Stw 2 mit Bedienungsstand
3 Winden W500/4 A B u C.
3 Kraftaggregaten KA300/2 A, B u C.

❝ In all the major cities of the American zone there is continuous building activity in bombed-out sections. Instead of removing all the bricks and stone rubble, contractors and concrete products firms are busy setting up mobile plants for crushing and screening the so-called *Trümmersplit,* or rubble.

A rather ingenious plant was observed producing a Jumbo brick in Stuttgart. The machine and the mixing plant were set up on one of the main streets of the city. The mixing plant was directly in front of a huge pile of crushed rubble, and the brick machine was built on the order of a travelling crane. The mold box is designed to make 60 Jumbo bricks at one time. As the machine operates it moves a few feet toward the mixer until the entire area of the street is covered with freshly made concrete bricks. These are then moved into stockpiles in front of damaged buildings or empty lots, and the same operation is repeated. The resulting output cannot be classed as a quality product and would probably not meet code requirements, but with reasonable care and supervision an acceptable product can be made to meet the existing emergency. **❞**

Field Intelligence Agency Technical Report 1123, Military Government for Germany [U.S.], June 1947

Germany: The Forgotten Miracle

It is a far cry from the prosperity of any American city in the 1980s, even the poorest, to the misery of Stuttgart in 1947. Germany at that time was defeated, partitioned, and under military occupation. One-third of her national territory was under the control of the Soviet Union, and the remainder was ruled in separate zones by the armies of the United States, Britain, and France. In the combined zones that were later to become West Germany — today one of the richest countries in the world — starving refugees from the east had swollen the population to a number one-third larger than in 1939. Of the 10 million houses in the region before the war, more than a quarter had been totally destroyed, and two-thirds had been damaged. Industry, commerce, transportation, agriculture, health care, and education had come to a halt in the chaos of defeat.

The seeds of the ingenuity displayed in postwar Stuttgart — elsewhere matched by the running of blast furnaces to make gas instead of steel and the fabrication of precast concrete flooring systems designed to fit between the walls still standing in bombed cities — were planted over a century before when the German states, newly unified under Prussian leadership, embarked on an expansionist foreign policy destined to culminate in the Great War of 1914. Germany's defeat four years later showed her crucial weaknesses as a world power. Compared with her opponents, she lacked essential raw materials, notably petroleum, rubber, and iron ore. Under the Treaty of Versailles she lost her only ore-bearing provinces, Alsace and Lorraine, to France and all her overseas colonies. Her resources for growth, limited before the war, were now hopelessly inadequate. This was the intention of the victorious Allies, who hoped by this means to limit Germany's power and influence in Europe.

The siege economy of the Great War had, however, wrought great changes in Germany's industrial base. Massive development of the chemical industry and heavily funded research into materials technologies had enabled her to find substitutes for many of the key resources she lacked. Because of the war and the years of poverty that followed, Germany confronted the oil crisis, the problem of wasteful industrial processes, and the disappearance of natural resources fifty years before any other developed country. She emerged with an entirely new kind of economy, one with unique, almost alchemical, powers of transformation and substitution combined with an extremely efficient mechanism of resource recovery, to which we will shortly turn. These developments had ominous political overtones, however. In the 1930s Germany embarked again on an expansionist foreign policy, which again culminated in war, this time a struggle fought to secure once and for all the agricultural land of Eastern Europe, the oil of the Caucasus, and the mineral resources denied by the Treaty of Versailles. Once again Germany lost, but by an even narrower margin than before. Because of the extraordinary efficiency of her economy — not because of the resources she temporarily seized — she was able for three years to resist the combined strength of the two postwar superpowers, Soviet Russia and the United States.

The amazing resilience of the German economy under siege was not lost on the victors of 1945. When her armies were finally defeated, the Allies sent teams of experts to sift through the wreckage of German industry and to bring home the secrets of its amazing productive power. The entire stock of patents held by German corporations and research laboratories fell into their hands. Between 1945 and the end of the military government in 1949, more than 17,000 technical reports on scientific, technological, and industrial developments in Germany were assembled by investigators in the Allied occupation zones. In the Soviet zone whole factories were dismantled and removed to the Soviet Union and its satellites.

Most of the vast quantity of information and equipment seized in the west was later made available to U.S. science and industry although to this day more than 100 Field Information Agency Technical (F.I.A.T.) reports remain classified. In some cases German paths of research were followed up immediately, in others not. A rocket-propelled guided missile fired by the Germans at London from a range of 200 miles became the cornerstone of a research and development program, which, a quarter of a century after the end of the war, placed American astronauts on the moon. A small fuel-efficient family car called the *KdF Wagen* ("Strength-Through-Joy-Car") was evaluted and dismissed as worthless by U.S. and British experts in 1946, only to become the Volkswagen beetle, the most successful imported car ever sold in America twenty years later.

Apart from isolated instances, the bulk of this German know-how was either painlessly absorbed or forgotten. Much of it related to conditions of scarcity, to material substitutions forced upon German industry by the war, and to painstaking and expensive alternative means of manufacturing or synthesizing what, in more fortunately endowed countries like the United States, was easily available. In a handful of countries some of the more advanced German methods were employed and even then with indifferent success, as in Peron's Argentina where efforts to develop a modern aviation industry under German tutelage fizzled out. Only in South Africa, equally isolated and starved of petroleum, was the valuable Pier-Farben coal hydrogenation process adopted and developed by a state-owned synthetic gasoline industry.

Low-Energy Conquest

Even without the distortions caused by enormous war production, the German economy was a strange hybrid: a combination of low-energy resources and high technological capability whose separate elements made little sense once the unifying principle of independence from all foreign resources, engendered by 100 years of European competition and conflict, was removed by defeat and partition. American studies[1] carried out in 1942, for example, showed that all the Axis countries possessed weak productive powers compared with their opponents, and these calculations led to a serious underestimation of their military strength. In 1937, according to the U.S. State Department, the total energy used in industrial production in Japan amounted to only 89 billion kilowatt hours and in Germany 234 billion kilowatt hours, compared with 911 billion kilowatt hours in the United States. By 1942, according to these same estimates, the Axis disposed of 650 billion kilowatt hours of productive energy including the additional capacity of their territorial conquests and the marginal powers of their allies in Eastern Europe. This figure, balanced against the 1,509 billion kilowatt hours available to the Allies at that time, showed that they could not possibly win a war based on industrial capacity. So it was to prove, but such calculations willfully ignored several anomalies. In 1940, when Germany, Austria, and occupied Czechoslovakia together mustered

barely 280 billion kilowatt hours of productive energy, they succeeded in defeating and occupying Poland and France and effectively neutralizing Britain even though the energy available for war production in those countries totalled 412 billion kilowatt hours. In fact, as postwar studies[2] showed, the entire military operations of the Axis powers during World War II consumed less natural petroleum than the peacetime U.S. market in 1940. When Hitler invaded Russia, he did so with more horses than tanks, and when the Japanese conquered Malaya and Indonesia and the Philippines, they did so with bicycles rather than with trucks.

At the time, the Germans were more technologically advanced than either the Italians or the Japanese, but compared with the United States all three were low-energy societies. The early German triumphs in Europe against the energy odds convinced them that they could defeat the Soviet Union when the energy balance was, for the first time, in their favor: 509 billion kilowatt hours versus only 236 billion. Yet they failed catastrophically, and the reason once again defies conventional energy logic.

Unlike Japan or Russia, Germany was a consumer society in the modern sense even before World War II. One of Hitler's undeniable achievements after 1933 was an almost magical reduction in unemployment, which in the democracies was notoriously high in the decade preceding the conflict. Nor was full employment in Germany solely the result of rearmament, which rose above 10 percent of the gross national product for the first time in 1938 and did not make serious inroads into the consumer sector until after the entry of the United States into the war.

As later economic studies have shown,[3] German arms production was not accelerated at the outbreak of war in Europe and remained intermittent until the first serious setback at the gates of Moscow led to the tentative imposition of overall planning. Even then, consumer production was not as drastically curtailed as in Britain or the United States. As late as October 1943, after Stalingrad, Kursk, the loss of North Africa, and the collapse of Mussolini's Italy, Hitler's armaments minister, Albert Speer, complained about unnecessary consumer goods output.

For example, we still produce in a year 120,000 typewriters, 13,000 duplicating machines, 50,000 address machines, 30,000 calculating machines, 200,000 radio receivers, 150,000 electric bedwarmers, 3,600 refrigerators, 300,000 electricity meters. . . . The production of stamping surfaces for ink pads is 6,200,000. The scissors production is . . . 4,400,000 a year.[4]

In the fall of 1941, when Hitler believed Russia was defeated, weapons production was reduced and soldiers were demobilized in anticipation of peace. Even after the Soviet winter counterattack, when the Germans temporarily regained the initiative with their deep thrust into the Caucasus, Hitler again attempted to switch priority back to the consumer sector and to prepare for the end of the war.

"Uses for the Useless"

How was it that Germany — a country lacking petroleum, with three-quarters of its iron ore deposits confiscated by the Treaty of Versailles, with no chrome, no nickel, no tungsten, no molybdenum, no manganese, no rubber, no zinc, lead, copper, or tin; and, furthermore, without centralized economic planning or any program for the enlargement of its basic production capacity or even any significant reduction in the output of consumer goods — was able to achieve one of the most remarkable periods of conquest in modern history?

The answer of course is not solely economic. It lies in part with the militaristic nature of the National Socialist state and the unpreparedness of its enemies, but it also depends to an astonishing degree on the state of development of German science and technology at the time, particularly in the chemical industry and in the field of resource recovery. Germany was the most energy-efficient country in the world in 1939, and as the pressure of the wartime blockade increased, it became more so. The secret of the Germans was *Verwertung des Wertlosen* — "finding uses for the useless."[5] For a time, it enabled them to fight a world war in the same way as the immeasurably wealthier United States was to fight its tiny war in Vietnam twenty years later — without apparent damage to its domestic economy. Even when the balance of power turned overwhelmingly against

Germany, this unequaled skill at resource utilization enabled them to endure loss and destruction for longer than their conquerors imagined possible.

The first indication of what "finding uses for the useless" might mean in terms of the German economy was seen in the last decade of the nineteenth century when the German chemist Karl von Linde succeeded in liquefying air and thus turning it into a raw material for industry. At that time there was near panic in agricultural circles in Europe at the impending exhaustion of Chilean nitrate reserves, then the basis of all artificial fertilizer. By 1912, building upon Linde's work, another German chemist, Fritz Haber, had succeeded in synthesizing ammonia from nitrogen, and with the cutting off of all nitrate imports after 1914, his method became a standard industrial process for the production of fertilizer. By 1938 German factories were synthesizing from the air six times as much nitrate fertilizer as had been imported before 1914.

Air liquefaction was later developed to yield economic quantities of the formerly rare gases helium, neon, argon, krypton, and xenon, which revolutionized the illumination industry. More importantly, it made possible the production of oxygen in bulk by the Linde-Frankl process, which in turn, made the gasification of coal a relatively cheap method of providing a whole range of chemicals from the plentiful German coal reserves. During the

1930s the Linde-Frankl process was developed into a network of more than sixty oxygen-producing plants capable of generating 6,000 tons a day. In the iron and steel industry the use of oxygen instead of air enrichment shortened furnace heating times and made possible not only a 25 percent increase in productivity but enabled more scrap to be mixed with pig iron, thus reducing the cost of the resultant steel.

Next came hydrogenation. Using the large quantities of hydrogen generated by the Messerschmitt process, in which steam was passed over hot iron particles, hydrogenation made it feasible to produce gasoline and various oils from both brown and bituminous coal. The German chemist Friedrich Bergius invented the first hydrogenation process during the Great War, but in 1930 it was superseded by the more productive catalytic method developed by Dr. Mathias Pier of I. G. Farben. Under the Four-Year Plan of 1936, whose aim was the achievement of raw material independence in iron ore, rubber, and petroleum, twelve new hydrogenation plants were constructed. After 1942 these produced — from brown coal, brown coal tar, petroleum residues, bituminous coal, and bituminous coal tar — all the aviation gasoline and most of the motor and diesel fuel used in Germany. By varying pressures and quantities, the Pier-Farben process could be made to yield a variety of products from gasoline and medium fraction oil to asphalt. At the peak of wartime output in 1944 hydrogenation was producing aviation, truck, and diesel fuel at an annual rate of over 1 billion gallons — about one-tenth the amount then being produced in the United States from natural petroleum reserves.

The production of oil from coal also made possible the German synthetic rubber industry, which, like its American counterpart, was based on the polymerization of butadiene, a substance obtained by the distillation of oil under pressure. Under the Four-Year Plan production of synthetic rubber rose from 22,000 tons in 1939 to 70,000 tons in 1942 and nearly 100,000 in 1943. The U.S. synthetic rubber industry, which was rapidly developed after the loss of natural rubber reserves in Southeast Asia in 1942, was based entirely on German

techniques acquired when Goodyear took over Farben's U.S. subsidiaries and patents.

Between the loss of the Alsace and Lorraine deposits in 1918 and the 1936 Four-Year Plan, the German iron and steel industry was almost entirely dependent on imported iron ore. In 1936 an enormous program for the exploitation of extremely low-grade ores was embarked on with the construction of a vast ore-processing plant at Salzgitter in Brunswick. With the same level of investment as went into the hydrogenation program, native pig iron production rose from 1.3 million tons in 1932 to over 10 million tons in 1940. The development of the Renn process, in which ores were mixed with fluidized coal dust and fed into special rotary furnaces, so reduced production losses that rock with an ore content lower than 1 percent could be processed economically. By the same means rare metals such as chrome, nickel, molybdenum, and tungsten were recovered from ores in which they existed in associate or even trace quantities.

New methods, such as the acid leaching of sandstone, were employed to produce quantities of vanadium for machine tools and low alloy steels. Electrolytic precipitation permitted the reprocessing of copper, lead, and zinc wastes left by earlier mining operations. Eventually, all imported ores were routinely analyzed for usable quantities of precious metals, including gold. All of these processes, pioneered in Germany as a result of chronic scarcities, have since been adopted by mining industries all over the world.

Nonferrous metal production too was the subject of intensive technical development, the most impressive result being the successful extraction of aluminum from native clay instead of imported bauxite. Several different processes were devised, all of which involved the electrolysis of clay to produce alumina followed by the crystallization of metallic aluminum. By 1938 a pilot plant was in operation in Germany producing 8,000 tons of aluminum a year, and, after 1942, all virgin aluminum was derived from this source.

The problem of copper supplies was never successfully overcome, for the deposits existing in Germany were speedily exhausted during the war, and new technologies were unable to compensate adequately in this case. The separation of copper from iron, lead, and zinc ores by flotation did permit the exploitation of some abandoned mines, but shortages were often made good only by the substitution of inferior materials.

Despite certain critical problems, such as the supply of copper, the Germans succeeded in synthesizing or finding substitutes for most of the crucial resources they lacked. From air, coal, and water their chemical industry was able to derive thousands of products, many of which were entirely new or could otherwise have been obtained only from abroad. The gasification of wood and coal generated whole ranges of feedstock chemicals. Fertilizers, dyes, pharmaceuticals, adhesives, paints, and synthetic fibers were made either from gases extracted from the air or produced by the hydrogenation of coal. Whole new families of liquid fuel, including oxygen, hydrogen peroxide, and nitric acid were used to drive turbines and rocket motors of enormous power. The combined efforts of advanced metallurgy and chemical engineering produced high-octane gasolines and methanol additives for high-compression engines, which by 1945 were producing four times the power of units of the same weight ten years before. Gas turbines developed for aircraft employed kerosene-based fuels to generate ten times the power of conventional piston engines, and rocket motors using a variety of solid and liquid fuels multiplied available energy by thousands.

Even before the war, alternative fuels were used extensively in transportation to reduce dependence on petroleum. The German state railways embarked on an electrification program in 1938 intended to cover the entire network within five years. Many trucks, buses, and street cars used steam power or gasoline engines converted to run on cheaply produced coal gas. Electric delivery vehicles were widely used in urban areas.[6] In the country, single-cylinder diesel tractors pulled trains of trailers, a technique which so impressed some American experts that efforts were made to introduce it into the United States after the war.[7]

The generation and distribution of electricity were expanded and increased in efficiency in another bid to reduce petroleum demand, notably by way of hydroelectric schemes and the exploration of long-distance, high-voltage transmission. One project, halted by the war, called for the transmission of two megawatts of power (equivalent in throughput capacity to ten freight trains of coal) from the Ruhr industrial district to Berlin, nearly 400 miles away. An even more visionary project involved the construction of a number of 1,500-foot triple rotor wind generators using high pressure electrolytic hydrogen production as a storage medium. Each unit was to have been able to generate 60,000 kilowatts.

Large-scale hydroelectric projects were undertaken using the Arno Fischer submerged turbine system, which made use of lower water gradients and cut costs and construction times by 50 percent compared with conventional Kaplan turbines. At Bleilochsperre on the Saale River in Thuringia, a complex of steam generators, pumped storage reservoirs, and water turbines combined to reduce the cost of electricity production by one-quarter. The reservoirs were filled by turbines run in reverse as pumps during off-peak hours and emptied to generate additional power during peak demand.

Some hydroelectric projects put forward during the National Socialist era were of scarcely conceivable size. The *Mittelmeer Senkung* (reduction of the Mediterranean) proposal advanced by the engineer Herman Sörgel[8] in 1938 called for the construction of three enormous dams in the Mediterranean Sea: one across the Straits of Gibraltar, another between Tunisia and Sicily, and the third across the Straits of Messina. These would have the effect of dividing the sea into two enormous lakes and cutting off the Atlantic inflow that presently occurs. Allowing the water level in these lakes to fall by evaporation would not only have created enormous new land surfaces for Spain and Italy (Germany's allies at the time) but also colossal hydroelectric potential, first at the proposed 330-foot drop from the Atlantic to the western lake and again at the 300-foot drop between the lakes themselves. The project, whose final goal was the fusion of the European and African continents, also embodied climatic advantages for north Western Europe because it was argued that the deflection of the Gulf

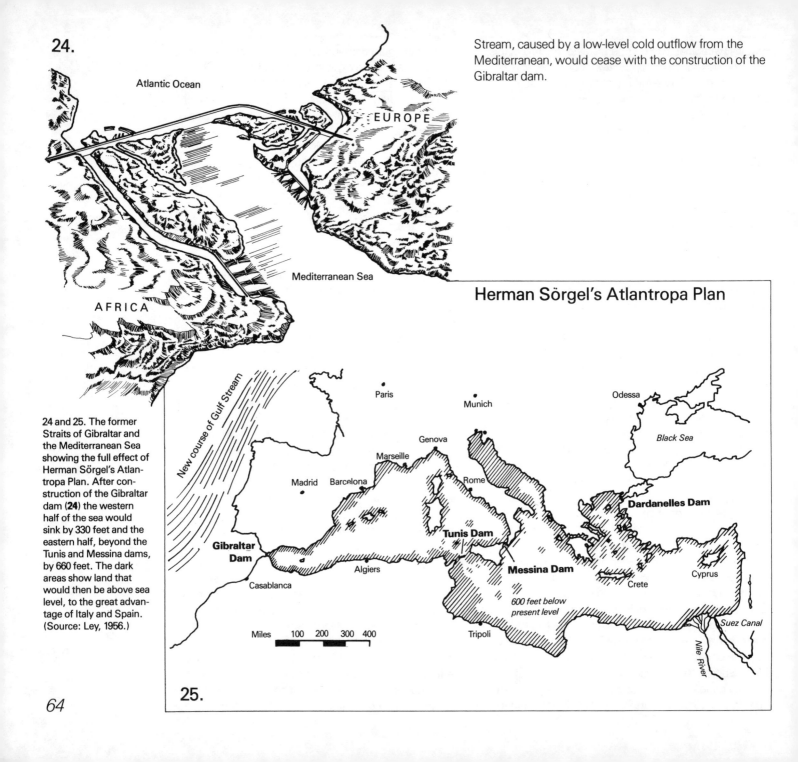

24.

Atlantic Ocean

EUROPE

Mediterranean Sea

AFRICA

Stream, caused by a low-level cold outflow from the Mediterranean, would cease with the construction of the Gibraltar dam.

24 and 25. The former Straits of Gibraltar and the Mediterranean Sea showing the full effect of Herman Sörgel's Atlantropa Plan. After construction of the Gibraltar dam (**24**) the western half of the sea would sink by 330 feet and the eastern half, beyond the Tunis and Messina dams, by 660 feet. The dark areas show land that would then be above sea level, to the great advantage of Italy and Spain. (Source: Ley, 1956.)

Herman Sörgel's Atlantropa Plan

New course of Gulf Stream

Paris
Munich
Odessa

Black Sea

Genova
Marseille
Rome

Madrid Barcelona

Dardanelles Dam

Tunis Dam

Gibraltar Dam

Algiers

Messina Dam

Cyprus

Casablanca

Crete

600 feet below present level

Suez Canal

Miles 100 200 300 400

Tripoli

Nile River

25.

The Role of Resource Recovery

As important as the many unique scientific and technical developments that the Germans applied to production and material substitution forty years ago was a resource recovery program so extensive and diverse that it might accurately be renamed a recycling culture. As in the case of agriculture, which had attained such efficiency that potato crops, for example, were more than three times larger for the same area of field in Germany as in the United States, resource conservation had been forced upon them first by the exigencies of the Great War. During the Weimar years many painfully established retrieval networks were allowed to fall into decay, but these were revived by the Nazis because of their contribution to national self-sufficiency. The extent of these operations makes interesting reading.

During the Great War, in addition to the conventional scrap industries based on iron and steel and other metals, there were government-sponsored reclamation schemes for used lubricating oil, paper, rubber, phonograph records, photographic film, kitchen scraps, pits and stones from fruit, coffee grounds, pine cones, nettles (special strains were developed for their fiber content), sea weed, acorns and horse chestnuts, cork and linoleum, tinplate, lamp sockets, electrical contacts, pen nibs, bones, bottles, obsolete coins, and rags. The conversion of rags into gun-cotton developed from a sideline in 1914 when 20,000 tons of reclaimed rags were used in this way to a major operation in 1917 when no less than 212,000 tons were so used and another 100,000 tons rewoven into textiles.

With the revival of these programs in the 1930s, the large number of paramilitary formations in National Socialist Germany came into their own. Unlike the United States today, the Germans made no attempt to mechanize resource recovery on a community or municipal scale; instead, they relied on large numbers of labor-intensive retrieval organizations feeding into a small number of large mechanized processing plants—similar in fact to voluntary aluminum recycling programs in the United States but with the important difference that no one was paid for the waste product itself since collection was deemed a national duty.

Within the area of greater Berlin the S.A., Hitler's stormtroopers, operated a free collection service for used lubricating oil, which was regularly picked up from garages and re-refined for further use. The *Hitler Jugend* organized the regular collection of coffee grounds from homes and restaurants and delivered bulk quantities to a Berlin factory where it was dried and washed with benzine to yield up to 16 percent of its dry weight in oils and waxes. The residue from this process found a ready market as a filler for phenolic resins in place of saw dust. The Hitler Youth also found unpaid employment in rag and bone collections, which took place during the first ten days of every month and were made the object of annual competitions. In 1937 they collected over 100,000 tons of animal bones, most of which were autoclaved to extract the bone fat and then fed into glue production. In 1934, the *Reichs-Luftschütz-Bund,* a volunteer air raid precautions organization, began the regular collection of wastes of all kinds from roofs and attics where a fire risk existed in the event of bombing attacks. Their first appeal in Hamburg produced 900 tons of steel and cast iron, 20 tons of nonferrous metals, 100 tons of rags, jute, and old carpets, and 8 tons of rubber. In the spring of 1936 the Wurttemberg S.A. collected 50,000 tons of scrap metal in the same way, all of which was hand-sorted and delivered to metal producers. In 1937 all these operations were brought under the control of a special government commission, the *Reichskommissariat für Altmaterial-verwertung,* which thereafter expanded the voluntary retrieval system to cover every aspect of the economic life of the country.[9]

With the coming of the war and the Allied blockade, resource recovery intensified. Despite manpower difficulties created by the mobilization of many of the volunteer organizations, a major shift from wood to straw as a raw material for cellulose production was achieved after 1940, with the straw collected and delivered by volunteer and conscript farm workers and prisoners of war. The disappearance of natural cotton, which had been imported, increased the need for waste textile collections and also led to an increase in the importance of synthetic fibers such as rayon, nylon (in Germany called "Perlon") and the production of textiles from jute, hemp, and nettles. Flax waste, used before the war for bedding cattle, was now woven into fabrics, and potato wastes were used as a replacement cattle bedding. Twine and coarse sacking were made from waste paper spun into fibers, and various types of paper and cardboard tube container replaced steel cans and drums. Natural cork was speedily replaced by a synthetic variety derived from fruit peelings.

With the onset of irreversible material shortages after 1942, more drastic measures were taken. Lack of copper for munitions led to the progressive replacement of copper wiring by iron in accessible supply cables and fixed installations. The Berlin Power and Light Corporation alone was required to surrender 20 tons of copper a month from this source. Large collections of disused and requisitioned cables were delivered to prisons where convict labor was employed to separate lead, copper, jute, and other materials.

Since the object of these economies was the maintenance of war production under increasingly difficult conditions, it was impossible to reduce electricity consumption itself in the most crucial areas of the economy although domestic supplies were rationed severely. At times in the aftermath of severe air raids, the frequency of the current was reduced in order to compensate for lost generating capacity even though this invariably led to serious problems with all electrical timing devices. On the Berlin S-Bahn rapid transit system, reductions of electric power frequency from 50 to 48 cycles caused the automatic signaling system to switch all indicator lights to "stop" so that it could no longer be used. When the frequency dropped below even this level, electric motors overheated and teletype machines became inoperable.

Within the munitions industries themselves major shifts in the raw material base were undertaken at a very late stage in the war to economize on petroleum, steel, and other scarce metals. Toluene, the oil-derived basis for TNT, consumed vast quantities of synthetic fuel: a typical bombing raid used up 10,000 gallons a minute. Consequently, the Germans switched to a substitute called "Myrol," which was obtained from methyl nitrate, which could be produced in large quantities by the hydrogenation of acetylene or the cracking of ethane. German aircraft production used increasing quantities of scrap aluminum and duralumin, obtained from airplanes shot down over the country. At the same time the aircraft industry began to use increasing quantities of the new plastics. "Dynal," a resin-impregnated paper pulp, was used for control surfaces, for access doors, and, experimentally, for whole fuselage and wing sections. By the end of the war, plans were well advanced for the construction of complete aircraft from foamed core plastics derived from wood or coal. These rocket-powered planes, armed with "Myrol"-charged weapons, would have used virtually no petroleum in their production or operation.

Such major transformations proved impossible to implement on the required scale under continuous bombardment, and the shift from petroleum was not achieved in time for the war production industries to withstand the systematic destruction of all the coal hydrogenation plants that took place in the summer of 1944. In the last desperate phase of the battle for Germany, even liquor distilleries and research establishments were compelled to produce small quantities of gasoline by distillation, but to no avail. Symbolically, the last offensive in the west, the Battle of the Bulge, was undertaken with inadequate fuel reserves and the hopeful issue of 10-foot sections of hose pipe to infantrymen to facilitate the syphoning of gasoline from captured Allied vehicles.

By the spring of 1945 Germany had become a fully mobilized country with no resources beyond desperate plans for petroleum-less and steel-less military might. The brief flowering of what truly was an alternative technology — perhaps best embodied in the oil-free rocket interceptor, made of plastic derived from wood or coal, hurling itself against the gas-guzzling dinosaur bombers of the Allies — proved futile in the end. Only the lessons of substitution and the habits of economy and ingenuity survived into the postwar world and made their own contribution to the famous West German *Wirtschaftwunder.*

The Meaning of the German Experience

With the passage of time it becomes increasingly obvious that many predictive factors were at work on the losing side in World War II. If we wish to study one possible pattern of breakdown for an energy-starved but technically advanced nation, we can see it in the fate of Germany, which went down with its blast furnaces glowing and its production lines moving to the very end. Short of that point there are organizational, if no longer technical, lessons in the extent to which the Germans did achieve economies and material substitutions — bizarre contrasts between the futuristic and the ancient, as when cart horses towed jet fighters to their dispersal points and autobahn gas stations sold bags of charcoal. Beyond these pointers too is the surrealistic parallel between the demands of total war then and the demands of the consumer economy forty years later. The same emphasis on production is there, the same colossal waste output, the same inexorable demand for vanishing raw materials. In the United States today there is no war of survival instigating conversion of all resources into military waste, but the endless appetite of the consumer sector does the same thing in a different way. Both consumer goods and weapons reach the scrap pile quickly, and the grim irony of the privations endured in Germany *simply to maintain the production of waste itself* has its analogue in the waste disposal problems thrown up by our own enormous productive capacity. Just as in Germany wrecked airplanes were thrown into furnaces to be melted down to make more airplanes, so today are auto hulks crushed and melted to make more automobiles. Just as in Germany shortages of fuel led to ingenious substitutions and whole new materials technologies, so in America does the rising cost of oil prompt solar research, the return of the electric car, and the exploration of hydrogen, ammonia, and alcohol as fuels, and continuing nuclear development.

The desperate efforts of German science, technology, and management to combat resource starvation — however induced — constitute a rich source of examples for the modern world, but there are limits to what we will allow ourselves to learn from it, not least because this epic struggle was undertaken with the evil and ruinous consequences epitomized by the collections of human hair and gold tooth fillings found in the Nazi concentration camps. No historian can disregard this deadly extension of resource recovery into slave labor and genocide; for the holocaust, like Hiroshima, has shadowed the whole meaning of technology from that day to this. The fatal confusion of means and ends that marred the efforts of those years will not in our lifetimes be disentangled.

Germany developed her recycling, ersatz economy as a result of the economic blockade forced on her in the Great War. Between the wars her capacities developed, as we have seen. During World War II they developed even more drastically but failed in the end to withstand the enormous pressure that built up after 1942. In the last three years of the war the overwhelming blows inflicted by the Allies swamped the adaptive genius of the German economy. It is true to say that taken together the forces of the Allies acted upon Germany as natural forces have acted on the global environment since the dawn of time; they were accelerated *evolutionary* forces. The Germans were forced to bend, and bend more, and finally break. Through the study of the German economy in the last years of the war, it should be possible to see how much a disciplined, high technology society *can* bend before it breaks.

Nearly a century before Hitler's war Charles Darwin wrote: "Man does not produce variability, he only exposes beings to new conditions of life and then nature acts on the organization and causes variability." The "new conditions of life" forced upon Germany produced extraordinary feats of adaptation and remarkable variations upon the technologies and methodologies employed elsewhere. The pressures of war forced the Germans to evolve, but they could not evolve fast enough or far enough to avoid extinction.

All this is of great importance if we believe that the energy crisis, "the moral equivalent of war," is an evolutionary force equivalent in its way to the massive armies brought to bear on Germany. If it is, then the threatened exhaustion of raw materials for America draws the German experience into sharp focus. Today it is everywhere accepted, often with misplaced pride, that the growth economy of the 1960s is a thing of the past and that the rate at which we consume energy can eventually be made to fall too. Alas, the corollary is seldom followed through; rising population, scarce energy, threatened raw material sources, inflation, and unemployment are recreating many of the conditions that existed fifty years ago — conditions that drove the Germans into a drastic attempt to achieve economic autarky — called in America "energy independence."

The same kind of fear of resource starvation and externally imposed poverty that influenced German policy in the 1930s is abroad in the United States in the 1980s. It is no accident that the prevention or exploitation of waste — finding uses for the useless — has assumed the character of another American frontier.

There is even a tiny talisman, a link between the last desperate products of Germany's besieged chemical industry and the consumer society that boomed in America for thirty years after the war. It exists in the high-strength hydrogen peroxide manufactured as an experimental U-boat fuel that was shipped to the United States for research in 1945. Because of problems with the stabilizing compound that the Germans had used, American military scientists found they could not work with it, so they sold it to the Buffalo Electro Chemical Company, which diluted it to a 3 percent solution and put it on the market in mouthwash and hair bleach.[10]

Notes

1. *Energy Resources of the World,* U.S. Department of State Publication 3428 (Washington, D.C.: USGPO, 1949). This data is based on updated 1942 strategic studies.
2. Editors of *Look* Magazine, *Oil for Victory: The Story of Petroleum in War and Peace* (New York: McGraw-Hill, 1946).
3. Notably Alan S. Milward, *The German Economy at War* (New York: Oxford University Press, 1965).
4. Quoted in ibid., pp. 106, 107.
5. This was the title of a book edited by Claus Ungewitter and published in Berlin in 1938 with an introduction by Hermann Goering. The book consisted of articles that had previously appeared in the trade journal *Die Chemische Industrie.* A British translation of *Verwertung des Wertlosen* was published by Crosby, Lockwood in London in 1944 under the title *Science and Salvage.*
6. Fritz Schumacher, the author of *Small Is Beautiful,* came to London from Germany in 1938 as an agent for German electric delivery vehicles.
7. The German technique was best exemplified by the Le Tourneau "Superfreighter" marketed unsuccessfully in the United States in the 1950s.
8. Herman Sörgel's book *Amerika, Asia, und Atlantropa* was published in Berlin in 1938. "Atlantropa" was his term for a combined Europe and Africa. The account here is taken from Willy Ley, *Engineer's Dreams* (London: Scientific Books, 1956).
9. *Science and Salvage,* p. 102.
10. This story is recounted in John D. Clark, *Ignition: An Informal History of Liquid Rocket Propellants* (New Brunswick, N.J.: Rutgers University Press, 1972).

5 Is a Keynesian Energy Policy Possible?

" If the Treasury were to fill old bottles with bank-notes, bury them at suitable depths in disused coal mines which are then filled up to the surface with town rubbish, and leave it to private enterprise on well-tried principles of *laisser faire* to dig the notes up again (the right to do so being obtained, of course, by tendering for leases of the note-bearing territory), there need be no more unemployment and, with the help of the repercussions, the real income of the community, and its capital wealth also, would probably become a good deal greater than it actually is. **"**

John Maynard Keynes, *General Theory of Employment, Interest, and Money,* 1936

Is a Keynesian Energy Policy Possible?

The above quotation is famous, and, lest like other users I should be accused of taking it out of context, it must be added that it is a figurative example used by Keynes to demonstrate that virtually any kind of public expenditure would have beneficial effects during a recession, such as the Great Depression, which was at its most severe when he wrote it. In effect Keynesian economics, or New Deal "pump priming," as it was called in the United States, did end the Great Depression, but not by burying banknotes. Rearmament for World War II served as well and perhaps as surrealistically in the context of a wise use of resources.

If the anticlimactic conversion of U-boat fuel into hair bleach marked the bitter end of the struggle for energy independence in Germany, it also heralded the age of Keynesian economics in America. There the immense public investment of the war years provided a launching pad for an unprecedented era of wealth, which was to last for more than a quarter of a century. When the Pax Americana finally began to come apart under the impact of the 1970s energy crisis, it was because supplies of the one domestic resource that had brought victory in 1945 finally began to give out. Rising demand, low prices, and the random dispositions of world geology took their toll and together determined that U.S. oil production would peak twenty-five years after the end of World War II. Thereafter, the United States, like its

former enemies, became dependent on imported oil or technological ingenuity. This crucial change ensured that of the three major threats to the new society of mass consumption — resource exhaustion, pollution, and nuclear war; the first, in the form of a looming energy famine, moved from the distant horizon to the foreground of political events. It was at precisely this point that the balance of political opinion in favor of public spending, a general continuation of New Deal methods, began to shift back towards a monetaristic conservatism not seen since the Hoover administration.

The first practical demonstration of the vulnerability of distant oil supplies occurred in late 1973 with the oil embargo imposed during the fourth Arab-Israeli war. From then on it became increasingly clear that as far as the United States was concerned, the existence of proven oil reserves was less important than the political stability of oil-bearing regions. In the Middle East, where the largest noncommunist-controlled reserves existed, political stability grew more and more fragile as the decade advanced. At the 1980 World Energy Conference held in Munich, pessimism over future supplies was universal, and the most optimistic paper claimed only that the United States might "muddle through for the rest of the century."[1] Most contributors to this international forum confined themselves to the consideration of invidious choices between nuclear power and a clutch of more or less unproven alternative energy sources.

Ten years after the first clear threat to its main fuel artery, the United States has still made no national policy response appropriate to the gravity of the situation. Despite media speculation, there have been no military adventures to secure oil-bearing regions (on the contrary, Iran, a major supplier, has been lost), nor has there been much of a technological initiative to develop alternate sources of energy under domestic control (on the contrary, nuclear power, the great technological prize of World War II, is now heavily discounted). The actual U.S. response has been to accept a decline in economic growth — a voluntary return to lower expectations than those entertained at any time in the last thirty years.

This turn of events is in stark contrast to the German resource starvation model of the first half of the century with its repeated resort to military force in order to secure strategic materials. Clearly, American consumer society does not behave as did Germany under the Empire or the Third Reich. At the level of national policy successive American governments since 1973 have weighed the evidence and finally advocated more or less a continuation of the status quo at the price of a steadily shrinking output of real wealth and a steadily rising incidence of paper pushing.

This national inactivity is instructive, but it is not the whole story. Whereas in old Germany or old Japan totalitarian social organization ensured that the individual placed the perceived good of the nation far above his or her own desires (only thus can the unspeakable and ultimately futile sacrifices of their peoples during the war be explained), the social structure of the United States today is far more sophisticated and fragmented. Here the perceived good of the individual not only takes precedence over that of the nation but actually frames the only language in which the real interests of the state can be discussed. Thus, the apparent absence of a *national* energy policy is, on the one hand, a true measure of the nontotalitarian nature of the American state and, on the other, merely the logical counterpart to the emergence of a strong and ambitious *individual* energy policy. The authentic response of a society of consumers to bad service

26. Past and projected U.S. demand for energy with no allowance for oil price increases or economies. These figures from the U.S. Bureau of Mines anticipated a per capita energy consumption of 26,000 kilowatt hours a year by the year 2000. (Source: Adler, 1973.)

Note: I quadrillion Btu equals 38 million tons of coal

Gas

Oil

Nuclea

Hydro

Coal

Quadrillion Btu

1930 1940 1950 1960 1970 1980 1990 2000

on the grand scale is: "Damnit! I'll do it myself."

To describe the search for individual energy independence in the United States as an antisocial, rather than a social, response to the crisis is not a criticism but a statement of fact. Self-sufficiency, the cry of every American with a solar collector, an acre of land, a windmill, or just a book about it, may be chimerical in national terms, but it appears tantalizingly close to those who dream of cutting loose from the crowd with an autarkic house, an electric car, or a hydroponic farm. There can be no country in the world so nationally dependent on imported energy where so many people believe themselves to be within reach of self-sustaining freedom: no culture whose intellectuals are so profoundly opposed to technology where future social peace is so inextricably entwined with technological development. If photovoltaic cells can power houses and feed their surplus energy back into the electrical grid, if revolutionary batteries can be developed that will run cars and trucks all day without pollution, if community wind generators can replace regional nuclear power plants, . . . then the American consumer can turn the tables on world crisis, sell electricity to the power company, forget about gas price hikes, shrug off big oil, *and* pay less in taxes.

No one should doubt the power of this vision. American consumers have set forth their energy requirements for the future in terms uncompromisingly based on patterns of suburban settlement and standards of middle-class mobility that were established in the years of petroleum prosperity before 1973. It is this genealogy which makes them see energy independence as a matter of lifestyles and hardware rather than renewed geopolitical struggle. For the moment the underpopulated single family homes of America, their driveways crammed with cars, trucks, motorcycles, boats, and lawn tractors, are hostage to foreign oil suppliers; but in the future the same way of life will be sustained by pieces of new technology sold like air conditioners today at Sears and Montgomery Ward. The tankers bringing oil across the ocean will be laid up; the Third World will keep its oil; the Americans will achieve energy independence.

The Myth of Energetic Monetarism

This description of the popular view of the energy crisis is not intended to be sarcastic. Consumption is not a trivial adjunct to life in the United States but the mainspring of its economy and the key to its political balance. Even if the energy policy framed by consumers for one another is nothing less than an immense catalogue of further demands upon energy, it is still better founded than government wisdom about economy and frugality. The honest consumer is a Keynesian, whatever his government says. His personal experience contradicts the notion that if we stop making swizzle sticks, reset thermostats, wear sweaters, ride bicycles, and ban nonreturn containers, we shall save enough oil to keep the price down. Such proposals have an ancient folk logic but a very modern catch. At the time of this writing, the 1,800 percent increase in world market oil prices since 1973 has already forced great "savings" in terms of reduced economic growth, but the consequence has been inflation, unemployment, crime, and real poverty: all the undesirable effects of economic recession deepening into depression. Decoupling economic growth from energy consumption stands revealed as yet one more theoretical smoke screen intended to obscure a slide back into the uncritical acceptance of social inequality characteristic of earlier times.

In the public mind, high energy consumption means rising standards of living, full employment, high wages, and social stability. Low energy consumption has come to mean high prices, falling standards of living, growing unemployment, and social unrest. Deep in their hearts — because the gap between the two events is bridged by living memory — the American people believe that the right government could *burn* its way out of the energy crisis just as the New Deal *spent* its way out of the Great Depression. In essence, this view says that economic growth is a thermodynamic reaction: without energy no heat, without heat no prosperity. Such thinking underlies much of the support for nuclear power, which is seen as the only source capable of generating heat on the requisite scale.

It is important in looking at these levels of response not to forget that, because the energy question is perceived economically rather than energetically, its underlying reality is invisible. In wartime Germany power outages and brownouts were a frequent occurrence (an evident energy crisis), but when power was available, it cost the same as prewar. In the United States today the lights burn as brightly as ever, but they eat up more and more of the gross domestic product in doing so. Attention is focused on money even though the reality is energy, and this economization plays a vital part in the growing acceptance of inflation that such measures as indexation, inflation accounting, and the deregulation of domestic energy prices (the last remaining Keynesian element in the energy economy) have brought about. Since 1973 the economization of the energy question has fostered the conventional wisdom that energy use must be cut back in order to slow demand and stabilize prices — the classical doctrine of the balanced budget expressed in the form of energetic monetarism.

Besides confirming the absence of a real energy policy, this conservatism is self-damaging. If economic responses to the energy crisis were the only kind permitted, it would still be possible to argue for a deficit-spending approach on the old New Deal pattern. But such thinking is now the exclusive preserve of the nuclear lobby where it is beset by a host of technical and political problems. In the absence of the nuclear option, what is left of a Keynesian energy policy? Surely only faster extraction and drilling, massive earth-moving for shale oil, and even more imported oil. This, opponents claim, would lead to limitless subsidies to hold down the consumer price of energy while its real cost rose steadily for political and geological reasons. It is the apparently insuperable barrier imposed by finite energy resources that prevents energy Keynesianism by forcing almost everyone to believe that there are no responsible growth options left — a conclusion that is reached much too readily. After all, the very essence of deficit spending is the achievement of net growth in the face of apparently fixed gross resources.

Take gold, for example, a commodity in shorter supply and of greater value than oil, a metal which was once believed to be as necessary a foundation for economic life as oil has become today. When the nation's currency was backed by actual gold reserves — as it was until 1933 — the quantity of paper money issued was limited by the promise printed on each dollar bill that a matching quantity of gold could be redeemed for it at any time. When the nation came off the gold standard, this promise was abrogated, and the government reserved the right to print notes in excess of the amount of gold held in reserve or, more correctly, to devalue the paper currency in proportion to the excess printing. The essential achievement of this process, once called "the new economics," was to decouple economic growth from the possession of gold by means of the production and circulation of what was, to all intents and purposes, a synthetic substitute.

In theory, just such a breakthrough could take place in the field of energy if a synthetic substitute for oil (the fossil fuel gold) could be produced and circulated in the same way. Such a development is perhaps unlikely as long as the task is interpreted literally, but a true parallel to paper money in the "the new economics" is not a miracle fuel so much as something quite different *that has the same effect.* Paper money is not a precious metal, but it is employed as a substitute for it. Similarly, the hypothetical substitute for oil need not be hydrogen peroxide or liquid oxygen or boron or ammonia, but any measure whose impact could be likened to that of a revolutionary low-cost fuel available in enormous quantities.

How the "New Energetics" Might Work

In Keynesian economics the theory of deficit spending in a depression argues that the economic growth generated through government borrowing rapidly increases the tax yield and thus services the debt incurred. One way in which "Keynesian energetics" might emulate this cycle would be if the same government borrowing took place in order to subsidize the cost of energy to consumers, with the same growth-promoting effect. The role of taxation would then be played by resource recovery, a technology or system of technologies that could retrieve a portion of the lost energy and resell it in order to service the debt incurred in holding energy prices down. The *effect* of this process would be akin to the introduction of a new miracle fuel, but no such fuel would be required. Rather, the overall efficiency of existing fuels would be increased, *not by producing energy but by reproducing it.*

Needless to say, the theoretical feasibilty of such a course does not guarantee that resource recovery could recycle sufficient energy or, by reducing waste, stretch its capabilities far enough to justify such a drastic change in policy. Just as the key issue in the "new economics" has always been the inflation that accompanies increased money supply (making more money do less work), so in the "new energetics" the critical factor would be the size of the real energy deficit incurred in holding to artificially low energy prices. As in all energy questions the acid test

of practicality here is the efficiency of the conversion process that translates fuel into useful work. It is at this point that economics, energy, and waste coalesce into an interdependent set of policy variables.

The Keynesian approach would undoubtedly lay great stress on the mining of agricultural and municipal solid waste for energy. In the former case, experiments have already shown that the pyrolytic conversion into gas of about a quarter of the nation's 500 million tons of crop residues, food wastes, and forest residues would produce a supply of energy equivalent to one-third of the fuel oil used in agriculture. This figure could undoubtedly be improved by organizing the retrieval of more remote and inaccessible supplies, in which case a reasonable estimate might be that resource recovery could cover half the cost of fuel to the industry.[2] In crude terms, therefore, agricultural fuel prices could be held down to half their present level to finance the development and distribution of the necessary technology to improve efficiency by the same amount. Alternatively, the same retrieved energy equivalent could be applied to the indirect petroleum consumption of agriculture by subsidizing the production of synthetic fertilizers.

The techniques available for the mining of municipal solid waste are more diffuse. The use of shredded and classified solid waste as a fuel extender for electric power generation is already operational in some cities, notably

Milwaukee where a 10 percent saving in coal has been achieved by the Wisconsin Electric Power Company. Pyrolysis too can produce saleable gas but at rates which are economical only on the basis of saved disposal cost. Methane production by anaerobic digestion of sewage sludge and hydrogasification to produce an oillike synthetic fuel are also under evaluation, as is a more complex process called bioconversion, which incorporates combustion, pyrolysis, and fermentation as a means of extracting variable quantities of fuel, protein, and chemicals from the organic fraction of solid waste.[3]

Taken together, all these techniques might produce supplies of *reproduced energy* equal to more than 20 percent of current national energy consumption on the basis of currently predicted performance. If their development were financed on the basis of a 25 percent reduction in energy cost to the consumer, the energy deficit entailed might rise no higher than 12 percent of current expenditure on imported oil, say, $15 billion of deficit spending to develop a new industry capable of employing thousands and reproducing the energy equivalent to 4.5 billion barrels of oil.[4]

This brief calculation shows how close in just one way the relationship between waste and energy could be, but there are other ways in which the operating efficiency of the American economy could be improved without reproducing energy or curtailing consumption. Part of any serious Keynesian approach to the energy question would be an assessment of the real economic efficiency, as opposed to the thermal, mechanical or electrical efficiency of the basic mechanisms that power any industrial society. Just as the velocity of circulation of money has as great an influence on the total credit available as does the sum of notes issued, so does the number of uses affect the economic efficiency of any source of power.

For work done, there is always a penalty paid in waste, for instance, in the line-loss between electricity generation and the point of consumption or the decline in quality of television reception at a distance from the transmitter. The efficiency of the mechanism is the reciprocal of the waste generated; when one is high, the other is low, and vice versa. As we saw in Chapter 2, traditional farming methods achieved poor productivity by modern standards but also very high waste utilization whereas mechanized agriculture produces more but cannot contain its own waste output. Clearly, efficiency here can only be calculated if there is a common scale to compare the value of the two products, for both have changed radically over the last century. This difficulty can be found in all attempts to assess real economic efficiency, as the following very specific example shows.

The gasoline engine, which was invented about 100 years ago, has become an absolutely fundamental mechanism in the modern world. Without it, petroleum would never have achieved its crucial importance as an energy source, and the issue of imported oil would certainly never have arisen. This being so, one would expect to find that its efficiency in converting fuel into work, after so many years of continuous development, would be very high. In fact, in a typical engine more than three-fourths of the energy contained in every gallon of gasoline is wasted.

A conventional four-cycle gasoline engine is, in the first place, an imperfect mechanism; 26 percent of the energy contained in its fuel is wasted because combustion is always incomplete, imperfectly timed, and plagued by gas dissociation and loss of heat to engine parts. A further 40 percent is lost because combustion temperatures must be kept below 2,000 degrees Fahrenheit to prevent the engine from seizing up or melting. The higher the combustion temperature, the more efficient the process, but more expensive materials to permit operation at higher temperatures would cost so much more that they are not economical. Furthermore, high-combustion temperatures mean hotter exhaust gases, which are also wasted. A further 5 percent is lost through the need to suck fuel into the cylinders on the intake stroke and to expel it through the muffler on the exhaust. Friction of the working parts of the engine takes away another 5 percent, and suboptimal gas flow resulting from choking, accelerator pumping, the curvature of manifolds and exhaust pipes, and carburetor metering takes away another 2 percent. The result is that of the

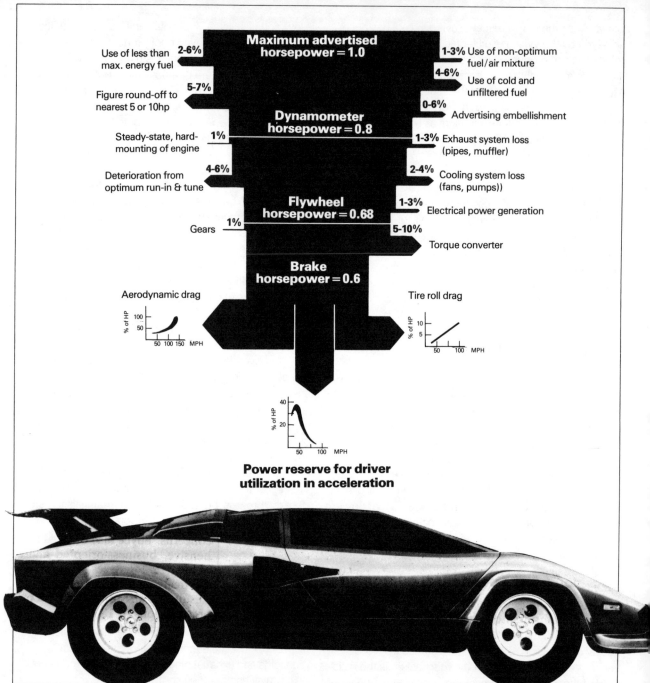

Maximum advertised horsepower = 1.0

Use of less than max. energy fuel 2-6%

Figure round-off to nearest 5 or 10hp 5-7%

1-3% Use of non-optimum fuel/air mixture

4-6% Use of cold and unfiltered fuel

0-6% Advertising embellishment

Dynamometer horsepower = 0.8

Steady-state, hard-mounting of engine 1%

1-3% Exhaust system loss (pipes, muffler)

Deterioration from optimum run-in & tune 4-6%

2-4% Cooling system loss (fans, pumps))

Flywheel horsepower = 0.68

1-3% Electrical power generation

Gears 1%

5-10% Torque converter

Brake horsepower = 0.6

Aerodynamic drag

% of HP
100
50
50 100 150 MPH

Tire roll drag

% of HP
10
5
50 100 MPH

% of HP
40
20
50 100 MPH

Power reserve for driver utilization in acceleration

27. Power wastage in modern automobiles. The low actual efficiency of the gasoline engine is clearly illustrated here. Its high relative efficiency is a result of a constant proliferation of uses. (Source: Hoffman, 1962.)

energy embodied in the gasoline fed into the engine, only 23 percent is delivered to the flywheel. From this must be subtracted cooling fan and pump losses, electrical generation loads, and the power lost on the journey through gears, torque converter, tire roll drag, and aerodynamic resistance to the actual performance of the vehicle on the road.

From this simplified account it can be seen that the gasoline engine is a complex and imperfect device that is more efficient at reducing fuel energy to heat and gas than it is at delivering power. Its wastefulness in this regard cannot be much reduced without raising its cost, which would in turn reduce its economic value. But it is this *economic* value that determines its real efficiency. Eighty years ago, when the gasoline engine was unreliable, even less efficient, and much more expensive in real terms than today's engines, it still outperformed animal haulage, steam power, and electric power. Even today, to convert 100 million gasoline-powered cars to electricity for a year's running would require a one-third increase in U.S. generating capacity — fifty times as much energy as is contained in the 8 billion barrels of oil that presently fuel those cars.

The balance between waste and economic usefulness is crucial in the consideration of a Keynesian energy policy, as it is in the evaluation of the gasoline engine. Actual practicality is always determined by relative rather than absolute advantage, as the examples of nuclear power and coal exploitation show. In the former case, the prospect of clean and unlimited electricity outweighs (at least in the minds of its supporters) the serious waste disposal problems associated with the nuclear option. In the latter case, the security of coal supplies justifies the high price in pollution that must be paid in order to extract energy from it. In considering the example of the gasoline engine, one must apply the same arguments: although a 5 percent increase in the mechanical efficiency of the unit itself would not significantly alter its operating economics, *added uses* of the gasoline-powered vehicle could swing the energy balance in favor of net growth within fixed outer limits and thus increase its economic efficiency much more.

A Keynesian House-Car Hybrid

onsider a hypothetical example: a gasoline-powered vehicle shaped like a large van, which could act as the kitchen, bathroom, and appliance center for a small dwelling. This mobile service core could be used for commuting, be driven to the supermarket — the purchases passed from trolley to refrigerator or freezer in the parking lot — and then driven home, plugged into the house, and used as a source of heat, light, and cooling during the owner's presence. The resultant vehicle might be larger than a car, have a larger engine, larger alternator, larger compressor, and several other accessories, but the total energy budget for the accompanying lifestyle might, nonetheless, be cut.

The savings on house construction costs would be considerable. If the vehicle carried an RV-style holding tank and was able to dump its contents at convenient intervals, say, whenever it refueled, the cost of a septic tank or sewage connection would be avoided. If it picked up water in the same way, the static house could become simply a lockable set of rooms with all the most expensive components transferred to the production line vehicle. Smaller than a camper but larger than a car, this hybrid would effectively shift the high-technology aspect of house building over to the high-technology automobile industry without any of the space or style problems encountered by the mobile home.

The energy implications of such a change would, of course, be extremely complicated to calculate in detail, but in outline terms some embodied-energy estimates will make the case. Embodied energy, which is dealt with in more detail in the next chapter, is the sum of energy invested in any product including the energy cost of extracting, processing, and refining the raw materials of which it is made, fabricating and assembling the various components, and delivering them to the consumer. Since the relative efficiencies of the construction industry and the automobile industry differ greatly — in the former one man/year of labor produces a $30,000 increase over material cost, and in the latter a $100,000 increase — the significance of the embodied-energy content of the basic product in each industry varies also. But the advantage of shifting the bulk of it into the high-value-increase industry is clear. Although the embodied-energy content of the hybrid vehicle would undoubtedly be higher than that of a typical compact car — perhaps twice as much at 500 million Btu (British thermal units) per unit — the embodied energy of the house component would certainly fall to one-third or less that of a conventional dwelling — say, 230 million Btu. On these figures the embodied-energy cost of the vehicle/house would be around 730 million Btu, as against 980 million Btu for a conventional house plus car — a saving of nearly 25 percent.

It is instructive to compare the embodied energy notionally saved by such an unorthodox approach with the same type of calculation applied to a solar-heated or solar-cooled house. Typically, the collectors, pumps, tanks, insulation, and control equipment installed in an otherwise conventional (in embodied-energy terms) house would involve some 400 million Btu additional to the 700 million, plus 250 million for the car: a total of 1,350 million Btu — virtually twice as much embodied energy.

There are, of course, many qualifications to be applied to this oversimplified case. Operating cost has not been considered, nor has the relatively short life of all motor vehicles compared with traditional houses; but once the possibility of trading functions between house and car is admitted, all these matters can be evaluated in a new context. The active life of the vehicle might be doubled by upgrading its specifications, or the life of the house might be halved. The point is that by treating the dwelling with its subsystems and the transportation needs of the occupant as functions of *one composite life-support system,* a large number of redundant parts can be identified, the removal of which might radically reduce the total energy budget for the same amount of work. This principle can be approached in different ways, but its tendency is always the same — to increase economic efficiency by multiplying uses and removing redundant (waste) parts.

By resource recovery and the elimination of systematic redundancies, it should be possible to operate a Keynesian energy policy that would permit considerable net growth even without major new energy inputs — a true parallel to paper money. There are both sophisticated and elementary ways in which it might be done, provided only that the impetus be created and the increased efficiency be required by reductions in energy prices to the consumer. The ingenuity required already exists and has been common parlance for some time. Richard Bender, for example, wrote ten years ago: "Why, since the bulk of what arrives as deliveries leaves as solid waste, can't these same trucks remove garbage? Since packaging decisions are part of the solid waste disposal problem, why can't one new organizational concept consider them together? Perhaps our soda can be packed in dog food — or fertilizer, or fuel."[5]

The real problem with such proposals is that while there may be no fundamental conflict between consumption and energy efficiency, the present consumer economy is geared to prevent them from taking place. As suggested in Chapter 3, our system facilitates production at the expense of reproduction: for every multi-use project, there are a thousand single use, irreparable, uncombinable, unrecyclable products on the market. Nor is product design and marketing the only powerful obstruction; labor practices discourage the removal of redundancy in services and transport, and whole complexes of industries defend threatened markets against technical innovations that could isolate and atrophy areas of energy waste.

The much discussed substitution of information technology for transportation is a case in point: the idea of a microcomputer in each worker's home and an end to tidal commuting promises enormous savings in energy. To take just one example, New York's Consolidated Edison's biggest load factor is mass transit, consuming 3 billion kilowatt hours every year. The computer idea is based on the same type of thinking that the Germans used when they planned to transmit electric power instead of railroading coal, and in their case an overwhelming defense need swept objections and vested interests aside. But in the absence of such compelling urgency, in an economy operated according to the so-called "Concorde fallacy" (the formation of policy on the basis of past effort instead of future gain), where is Bender's "new organizational concept" to find its necessary support? — only by the construction of a bridge between the instinctively correct energy policy of the American consumer and the necessary regulatory powers of the federal government. It is here that the whole question of the design-controlled evolution of all consumer products finally emerges in its proper context, a matter to which we shall return in Chapter 8.

Notes

1. Nicholas Hirst, "Adding Up the Earth's Oil Reserves," *The Times* (London), 15 September 1980. A less optimistic paper delivered by a representative of Electricite de France predicted that Third World oil demand alone would exceed all present oil demand within thirty years.

2. These estimates are taken from J. A. Knight, J. W. Tatom, et al., *Pyrolytic Conversion of Agricultural Wastes to Fuels* (Atlanta: Georgia Institute of Technology Press, 1974).

3. Steven J. Hitte, *Anaerobic Digestion of Solid Waste and Sewage Sludge to Methane* (Washington, D.C.: Environmental Protection Agency, 1976).

4. Annual cost to the United States of importing oil taken at $100 billion for the five years 1980–1985.

5. Richard Bender, "Pipe Dreams," *Architectural Design* (London), March 1972.

6 Waste Construction and Energy Economics

❝ It sounded like a winner when the Marathon Rotary Club began an artificial reef made of tires. It would let game fish feed close to shore, and small boaters wouldn't have to go three miles out for good fishing. But the project has become a naturalist's nightmare, says Richard Helbling, a biologist with the Florida state Department of Environmental Regulation. The structure that was to become the reef has broken apart. Tossed by the ocean currents, concrete slabs and bundles of tires are smashing fragile coral and mowing down the turtle grass where baitfish, grouper and snapper search for food. . . . The start of the project was marked by a visit of the Goodyear blimp. The tire company made a promotional film touting the display of environmental awareness. **❞**

Miami Herald, May 29, 1979

Waste Construction and Energy Economics

The use of waste material in construction is not a new idea. Two thousand years ago the Romans used the slag from iron workings to form the core of roads in mining areas. In the Middle Ages courtyards and squares in Europe were sometimes paved with the bones of cattle; and for generations farm workers' cottages were roofed with waste corn stalks, just as in the United States farmers' barns were painted with a mixture of surplus milk and rust. Even the word "window," derived from "wind eye," refers to the old rural practice of setting a cask into the wall of a dwelling, whose floor, more often than not, was made from a mixture of clay and cattle dung pounded flat.

With the coming of the Industrial Revolution a different kind of waste began to be used. Worn-out chains and iron cables were stretched as reinforcement in some of the earliest concrete buildings, and machine-produced bottles and cans began to appear in the structure of houses built in Alaska during the gold rush and later during the mining boom in the West. One bottle house, built in Rhyolite, Nevada, in 1912, survives to this day as a tourist attraction in what is now a ghost town.

The two great wars of the twentieth century created mountains of waste, much of which later was used one way or another in construction. After World War I iron sheets rolled for ship building were used as siding for public housing projects in the north of England, and precast concrete elements developed for field fortifications by the French were later used for lintels and floor slabs in a variety of buildings. In Europe after World War II gasoline cans filled with earth were sometimes laid like bricks in cement mortar to build houses, and perforated metal strip (used by the military of several nations for advanced roads and airfields) was pressed into service as siding, reinforcement, and structural steelwork all over the world. Many materials developed to provide bomb shelters in Britain were quickly adapted for use in agricultural and light industrial buildings.

With the coming of the years of affluence, all these thrifty techniques fell into disuse in the developed countries. But in the Third World, where the global conflict had for the first time exposed societies of subsistence agriculture to the full impact of advanced technology, the legendary wastefulness of modern armies laid the groundwork for a living tradition of waste building. The process of global urbanization, which began in the postwar years and reached a crescendo a quarter of a century later, seized upon the salvage methodology to such effect that in the once-colonial nations of Africa, Asia, and South America millions came to spend their lives in shacks constructed from the detritus of the Western container and packaging industries. The billions of cans, drums, boxes, crates, and other containers in which the produce of the wealthy nations was transported over the globe soon became the basic building materials of the dispossessed.

In the fullness of time this essentially amateur technology was found to be a proper subject for academic study. Most of the developing countries were excessively dependent on imports of all kinds, especially building materials, the purchase of which absorbed a large proportion of their available foreign exchange. With the coming of the energy crisis, whole ranges of adhesives and binders used in modern construction, derived as they were from petrochemicals, became too expensive to use, as did steel, concrete, and many other basic building elements. Using the methodology of the poor, the architects and builders of the Third World turned to

waste in developing their own materials industries. Abundant agricultural wastes, such as rice hulls, jute stalks, ground-nut shells, sugar cane residues, and coconut husks, were examined for their construction potential, which, in many cases, turned out to be considerable.[1] Rice hulls proved to be useful as a source of silica for the manufacture of pozzolana cement and also as a raw material for the production of adhesives. Chipboard and other rigid sheet materials could be made from jute stalks or sugar cane waste; water-resistant building boards were made from coconut fiber and corrugated roofing sheets from cement-reinforced fibers of several kinds. Straw and similar crop wastes were converted into structural members by the Stramit process (pioneered in

28. The traditional use of waste materials in construction. This sod cottage, still in use in England in the early years of this century, was made of mud with a roof of straw and the chimney, to the left, formed from a barrel.

29. A bottle house built in Nevada in 1912. Only a decade after the invention of the Owens rotary bottling machine, which revolutionized bottle production, the product was so plentiful that it could be obtained more easily than conventional building materials in frontier towns. This house is still in existence, as are a few others built in Alaska, Australia, and New Zealand.

30. As part of a United Nations program in Dubai, members of the McGill Minimum Cost Housing Unit set up a small sulfur block production plant in 1978 and built prototype structures like this one for evaluation. The prospects for conversion of much of the sulfur extracted at refineries from Dubai's oil into building blocks appear good.

Germany), using pressure and heat generated by the burning of quantities of the same material.

Lack of development capital and of a suitable engineering infrastructure has so far prevented these new techniques from dominating the construction industry in underdeveloped countries, but in those few with oil wealth the shape of things to come can be clearly seen. Dubai, for example, a small oil exporter on the Persian Gulf, is experimenting with sulfur concrete — with the aim of diverting the 100,000 tons of sulfur extracted from crude oil every year by each of its refineries into construction work. Given the passage of time and a consistent policy in this regard, the use of wastes to offset the cost of imported building materials may soon have a significant effect on the balance-of-payments situation in many developing countries.

While the past decade's massive increases in the price of oil had by no means the crippling effect on the American economy that they did on those of the developing countries, their domestic impact was severe. In a sense, heavy investment in offshore drilling and the construction of the Alaskan pipeline were facets of a partial return to developing status, and with this return came a new interest in energy-saving techniques of all kinds, including the material substitutions promoted by technical advisers in the Third World. As the decade advanced, not only did investment from oil-rich Middle Eastern states find its way back to the United States but also some of the ersatz building technology that had grown up in the poorer countries.

Government Surveys: Some Background Data

Beginning in 1974 the Department of Energy embarked on a number of computer studies intended to produce a "snapshot" of energy movement through the U.S. economy in a typical year. The final product was a 1977 report entitled *Energy Use for Building Construction* (*EBC*), which offered a detailed breakdown of the direct- and embodied-energy demands of the construction sector ten years before. According to its findings, construction emerged as a large-scale energy user, responsible for 10 percent of the 70 quadrillion Btu of energy consumed nationwide in 1967. Of this 10 percent, about half was used in new building, 40 percent in engineering sectors such as highways, oil wells, gas pipelines, dams, and waterways, and 10 percent in maintenance and repair. Within the new building category, manufactured materials and products accounted for 70 percent of the energy used, direct energy supplied to building operations (refined petroleum products, gas, and electricity) for another 15 percent, and construction-related overheads for the remainder. Dependent on the type of building, the embodied energy represented by manufactured materials and products could consume 2 million Btu per square foot—as in the case of science laboratories—or only 500,000 Btu per square foot in the case of warehousing. Single family detached housing, the largest single category with the largest completed square footage (30 percent of all enclosed floor area) accounted for no less than 700,000 Btu per square foot over more than 1 billion square feet of new domestic construction. All told, the construction sector was capable of consuming the energy of 2 billion barrels of oil every year.

At the time of the *EBC* report, a quite different study was published by the Department of Energy. Entitled *Survey of Uses of Waste Materials in Construction*, this document examined the total volume of waste generated by the U.S. economy in terms similar to those found in Chapter 2 of this book and compared these quantities and materials with the amount of inert filler, matrix, and binder consumed by the construction industry. The results were staggering. While 3 billion tons of mining, agricultural, industrial, and consumer waste was expelled each year by the operations of the economy, no less than 1.5 billion tons of sand, gravel, crushed stone, gypsum, slag, and cement were dug out of the ground for use in construction over the same period. In theory, it looked as though the industry could learn to absorb up to half of the nation's waste in the production of capital goods—a quantum leap in efficiency more than equal in effect to the negative impact of the energy crisis. Unfortunately, as was apparent to its authors, such a conclusion ran counter to a number of disconcerting facts. Although it was true that two-thirds of the waste material produced by the U.S. economy took the form of mining waste, it was equally true that, in general, mining areas were remote from areas of urbanization so that large transportation costs would have to be added to the already considerable cost of handling the waste rock and tailings again. Furthermore, most significant mining wastes were already amassed in such volumes that no conceivable construction project could make inroads into the quantities available — even less so if the promised exploitation of oil shale and doubling of coal extraction (which would contribute vast additional wastes) took place in the future. Preferential freight rates, tax abatements, and other economic inducements might make it advantageous for the construction industry to use mining or agricultural wastes wherever possible; but the national and, to an even greater extent, local disproportion between supply and demand represented an immovable stumbling block. To make it economical for the construction industry to use even 500 million tons of waste rock a year would cost more in foregone revenue and increased transportation costs than it would save — a conclusion that remains valid today.

In any case, the report was uncertain what the net saving would be. Part of the proposal concerned the use of mining wastes in landfill in place of the municipal solid waste and demolition waste presently trucked from municipalities. This idea was sound as far as it went because the use of such inert materials certainly would obviate the increasing difficulties that were already emerging in the reclamation of landfill areas as a result of water pollution, subsidence, and flammable gas production resulting from the decomposition of municipal solid wastes underground. But if urban wastes generated near landfill sites were to be rejected in favor of mining wastes trucked from hundreds of miles away, then the problem was not so much being *solved* as *shifted* from one sector to another. On the one hand, every copper mine produced more waste rock and tailings than neighboring construction could absorb; on the other, existing methods of disposing of energy-intensive urban wastes were threatened by a kind of waste busing program. In theory, 50 percent of the nation's trash pile *could* be used in construction, but under present circumstances such a departure could not square with economic efficiency. Before such a thing could be done, virgin supplies of comparable inert construction materials would have to be exhausted, or the whole geographical relationship of urban areas to mineral reserves would have to revert to the balance that obtained in preindustrial times when

power could not be transported more than a few hundred feet.

Underlying these logistical reasons for the inability of the construction industry to profitably adopt mining waste lies the problem presented by the pattern of energy consumption within the industry itself, which in many ways militates against all use of waste materials. Despite its low productivity and long product life, construction is heavily weighted toward energy-intensive components. As the *EBC* report showed, 70 percent of the energy annually used in the production of buildings is consumed by the manufacture and delivery of purpose-made building materials and products derived from steel, wood, aluminum, glass, and plastics. Of the remaining 30 percent, half is consumed in the form of asphalt for parking lots. Only a very small percentage of the energy swallowed up in construction is actually accounted for by sand, gravel, or any of the other inert fillers or extenders used in building. Their energy intensity is, in fact, so low that the real target for energy conservation through the use of mining wastes is perhaps 5 percent of the construction sector total — a mere 360 trillion Btu or 12 million kilowatt hours, little more than the annual energy consumption of a small aluminum recycling plant.[2] Clearly, unless the construction industry itself is revolutionized, solving the mining waste problem in this way will only intensify energy demand.

In one sense it will always be logical to use that which is thrown away as of no value in place of that which must be won from the earth and fabricated at great expense. In another sense such substitutions are never as straightforward as they seem. The performance of the waste, the cost of transporting it, the quantities in which it is available or needed, the modifications necessary at all stages of the production process to accommodate it — all of these conspire to undermine the "obvious" advantage. The sum of these difficulties is called inertia, the structural resistance to change built up by any established methodology. In the construction industry this inertia has a tangible element, the long life of the building itself, and this factor is of overwhelming importance in any attempt to change it.

The Effects of Inertia in Construction

If energy saving is to be the measure of success in the use of waste in building, then the principal obstacle must be the fact that most energy will be consumed by buildings that already exist — as opposed to those that are in production. This can be simply demonstrated by comparing the annual production of houses with the number of houses already occupied. Even in a record year, when more than 2 million new houses are built, this only amounts to 3 percent of the inhabited dwellings in the country, which means that no less than forty years of house construction is necessary before any major change in construction methodology applies to the majority of houses. In relation to consumer products in general this situation is unique. Automobiles, for example, have an average life of less than ten years and are produced in such volume that a federal requirement for, say, 40 mile per gallon mileage ratings can be enacted into law and apply to most of the cars on the road in only six years.

The low annual production rate of buildings means that attempts to improve their operating energy consumption — analogous to improvements in fuel consumption for cars — must overwhelmingly be based on retrofit technology. This fact alone shows the inefficiency and unresponsiveness engendered by the low productivity of the construction industry. *If the 100 million cars in America had to be individually returned to the dealers who sold them in order to improve their gasoline con-sumption by 5 miles per gallon every few years, the cost would be astronomical; it would not be considered feasible by the automobile industry. That it is considered feasible for buildings tells us a lot about the relative inflexibility of energy demand in the construction sector.*

Compared with buildings, cars are practical, functional devices with relatively objective criteria of value. The extent to which cars are endowed with nonfunctional attributes (rarity or opulence, for example) merely serves as an indication of how much more so are buildings, particularly houses, which have come to serve as a medium of investment and exchange in a manner that owes almost nothing to their functional performance and almost everything to their location and scarcity.

Compared with cars, or airplanes, or even refrigerators and washing machines, the performance per pound of most common building types is dismal, and this too contributes to inertia in the construction industry. During the 1970s a number of attempts were made in the United States to launch building materials (as opposed to fillers or extenders) derived from wastes. "Envirite," a foamed glass and animal manure building block, and "Glasphalt," a crushed-glass surfaced road-making material, were both cheaper and more energy efficient than the conventional products with which they were in competition, but neither was ever used for more than a demonstration project. Architects and other building material specifiers make their decisions on other grounds than energy efficiency, except in relation to a small range of very specialized building types.[3]

It is a function of the long life of buildings that their operating cost in energy terms greatly outweighs their initial construction cost. Given a forty-year life, the average domestic building will consume 80 percent of its life-cycle energy servicing the heating, lighting, and air conditioning requirements of its occupants and only 20 percent in the course of its own construction. This imbalance too originates in the poor productivity of the construction industry and reinforces its built-in tendency toward improvement by retrofit rather than modification at production stage. The resultant condition, where no production

modification can affect more than 20 percent of the building's life-cycle budget, not only inhibits innovation in construction but perverts the pursuit of energy efficiency in building as a whole; for the concern with operating costs that derives from low productivity feeds into new construction in the form of a tendency to cut operating costs at the expense of capital costs. Ambient-energy-powered buildings, such as solar houses, are examples of this when they attempt to avoid the operating expenses of twenty years by means of one down payment: a piece of alternative technology sleight-of-hand that makes no sense energetically and only appears to work appears to work economically because inflation accounting is still in its infancy.

Such a statement may seem heretical, but it is a fact that what solar houses really do in energy terms is to draft hundreds of tons of high-embodied-energy materials such as plastics, glass, aluminum, copper, steel and microelectronics into otherwise conventional buildings as a form of speculation against rising operating costs in the future. The whole process works very much like a fixed-interest mortgage in inflationary times — to the advantage of the borrower but to the disadvantage of society as a whole. Just as a house bought on a 9 percent mortgage over 25 years represents good value when interest rates top 20 percent, so does 400 million Btu of solar technology bought at 1977 prices look good in 1987, when other forms of operating energy cost twice as much as they did ten years before. The catch is that someone else is paying for both.

Table 12 represents an attempt to quantify the impact of reduced operating cost upon construction cost by way of measured energy intensity. It assumes an annual production of 1,100 million square feet of single family housing and accepts the *EBC* report estimate of 700 million Btu of embodied and direct energy for each house. The additional embodied and direct energy attributable to solar technology for water and space heating or cooling is averaged at 400 million Btu per house. It should be clearly understood that this figure does not apply to so-called passive solar houses, which derive their improved thermal performance from orientation and

31. Floor tiles, wall tiles, and acoustic ceiling tiles shown here, in addition to the blocks in the foreground, are all building materials developed by the Glass Container Corporation of Fullerton, California, to incorporate quantities of waste glass. Though used experimentally, none of the nine has been commercially successful. The most notorious was "Envirite," developed by John D. Mackenzie of UCLA, which used a mixture of animal dung and crushed glass to produce a lightweight, foamed block.

94

mass under glass—although even here there is undoubtedly an energy price to be paid—but to houses with solar space heating using flat plate or focusing collectors, pipework, pumps, heat storage, blowers, control gear, and the not-inconsiderable supporting structure required by this equipment. Although the precise requirements in terms of energy-intensive copper, aluminum, steel, glass and plastics of such houses vary in different parts of the country, 400 million Btu is a typical figure for a Northern or Midwestern state with a long heating season, reflecting the quantity of energy that would be used in the manufacture and assembly of these materials and the direct energy requirement of transportation, assembly, and fixing.

As the table shows, each solar house could cost more than half again as much as a conventional house in embodied energy, even if this increase was not immediately reflected in a proportionately higher cost. Delays and distortions in the relationship between energy costs and material prices, which are clearly identified in the *EBC* report, sooner or later resolve themselves under pressure of demand, and this temporary cost immunity could not be maintained. Even simple weatherization programs with their need for insulation and caulking materials show feedback effects on material prices. How much more dramatic would be the inflationary effect of a nationwide solar housing program? And how disingenuous are those who endeavor to distort energy economics even further by demanding grants and tax allowances to make cheap that which already trades at far below its true energy price?

If the energy accounting in our economy was corrected continually for diminishing energy reserves, as interest rates are corrected in a variable-rate mortgage, such attempts could not succeed. The cost of embodied energy would then equal the cost of operating energy, and, although both could be modified in response to improvements in real efficiency, the cost of a year's electricity could be equated with the cost of an energetically similar quantity of asphalt shingle roofing or a load of ready-mix concrete. We have OPEC price increases to thank for what inflation accounting exists in the energy

Table 12. Impact of Solar Technology on Annual Energy Demand for New House Building

Single Family Housing	Energy Demand in a Typical Year
Conventional single family housing	770 (trillion Btu)
With 25 percent solar housing	879 (up 14%)
With 50 percent solar housing	990 (up 28%)
With 100 percent solar housing	1,210 (up 57%)

Source: Author's estimate based on *EBC* figures for embodied energy of materials used in typical solar homes

field. In all other respects we continue to operate a fossil fuel subsidy that conceals the fact that to try to control operating costs in future by means of unlimited construction cost in the present is a parody of all consumption: it is as though a person, fearful of the rising price of food, resolved to eat a lifetime's supply at one sitting.

The present cost advantage that a solar house embodying 80 percent of its life-cycle energy demand and amortizing only 20 percent of it enjoys over a nonsolar 20/80 house is a function of the as-yet-undeveloped solar market. Once demand builds up, real prices will not be far behind, and solar technology will reveal itself to be not a solution to the energy crisis, but a part of it: subject to the same laws of supply and demand as other fuels. Nor is it very likely that the direct conversion of solar radiation into electricity will change this picture. At the time of writing, photovoltaic electricity generation costs about fifteen times as much as conventional methods, and considerable extrapolation of inflationary trends is necessary to make figures like $5,000 per kilowatt hour look promising for any but the very rich.[4]

It is of course bad logic to attempt to demolish a case on the basis of immediate and complete substitution. No doubt the encroachment of flat plate and photovoltaic technology will be much more gradual that its proponents claim, or its opponents fear. Nonetheless, there is no avoiding the deduction that any shift from operating cost to first cost will intensify energy demand and push prices up faster than would otherwise be the case. A large-scale solar program using today's technology would have the effect of increasing the percentage of all energy consumed by domestic construction from 10 to nearly 20 percent—with consequences that would undoubtedly include the erasing by price increases of any apparent advantage gained. It is of course true that solar technologists might counter this pressure from real costs by material substitutions and improvements in efficiency, and any such tendency should be encouraged, but such innovations would have to be weighed in the balance against an overall energy equation that would simultaneously admit many different ways to make the same savings. Once a true energy budget is revealed —one in which embodied and direct energy are debited alongside operating costs—the spectrum of possibilities enlarges enormously, and it is here that economies in material cost, irrespective of energy systems, can offer more for less in a decisive way.

Embodied Energy in Some Typical Assemblies

In order to approach the energy equation by way of its embodied as opposed to its operating component, it is necessary to apply the *EBC* evaluation technique to the issue of waste materials in construction. To replace sand with a phosphate sludge derivative or gravel with copper tailings or waste rock is, as we have seen, of little value as far as the overall energy budget for construction is concerned because the substitution of fillers and extenders will affect less than 5 percent of construction energy use. There are, however, many energy-intensive wastes that might be employed in the industry as substitutes for more important components in its energy budget, among them the disused products generated by the container and packaging industries, the tire companies, the textile companies, and many other branches of productive industry. Because of their high-embodied-energy content these wastes have long been the target of recycling campaigns, but the volume in which they are produced has so far defeated all measures. Even the valuable aluminum can evades recapture three times out of four. What would be the result of employing these wastes in construction?

Table 13 gives approximate embodied-energy values for five short-life products and three building elements. This table shows a reasonably close relationship among all these products in dimensional terms. Six beverage cans occupy about the same volume as a con-

Source: Hannon, 1972; and Hannon, Stein, et al., 1977

Table 13. Embodied Energy per Unit for Some Common Products

Product	Btu
Steel beverage can	4,300
Aluminum beverage can	6,500
Glass beverage bottle	7,800
House brick	14,000
Concrete block	30,000
Car tire	1,000,000
Downsized car	250,000,000
Single family house	700,000,000

crete block and account for 80 percent of its embodied energy whereas (on average) two bottles equal one brick and take 40 percent less energy to make. The relationship between the embodied-energy content of cars and houses in their entirety was the subject of speculation in the last chapter. Only tires are anomalous in their short life, high-volume production and enormous embodied-energy content.

As we shall see in the next chapter, techniques for building with these wastes already exist, making it possible to compute their embodied-energy cost. Furthermore, since the *EBC* report provides detailed embodied-energy analyses of several typical construction

Source (Tables 14 and 15): EBC report

Table 14. **Energy Analysis of Brick on Wood Frame Wall**

	Btu per Square Foot
Bricks	105,000
Building paper	—
Plywood sheathing (½ in.)	5,779
Gypsum wallboard (½ in.)	5,297
Batt insulation (3 ½ in.)	6,860
Wood framing (2 in. by 4 in. at 16 in. o.c.)	3,486
Total	126,422

Table 15. **Energy Analysis of Wood Shingle on Wood Frame**

	Btu per Square Foot
Wood shingles	7,315
Building paper	—
Plywood sheathing (½ in.)	7,705
Gypsum wallboard (½ in.)	5,297
Batt insulation (3 ½ in.)	6,860
Wood framing (2 in. by 4 in. at 16 in. o.c.)	3,486
Total	30,663

assemblies in current use, it is possible to make some preliminary comparisons between conventional methods and experimental waste construction techniques. The overall value of such comparisons can also be assessed by means of the *EBC* report because it provides a sector breakdown of energy use that shows in single family housing, for instance, 78 percent of all embodied and direct energy goes into general construction (foundation work, walls, roof, doors, windows, and finishes) where such wastes could readily be used; and only 22 percent is attributable to mechanical equipment, electrical installations, and site overheads. For this reason the following comparisons, despite their rudimentary and incomplete nature, are of some predictive value in assessing the overall impact on construction energy consumption of these and other energy-intensive wastes even though

32. Brick on wood frame wall.

33. Wood shingle on wood frame wall.

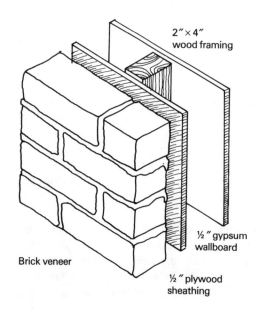

2″ × 4″ wood framing

½″ gypsum wallboard

Brick veneer

½″ plywood sheathing

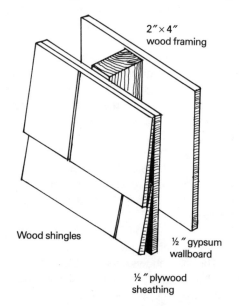

2″ × 4″ wood framing

Wood shingles

½″ gypsum wallboard

½″ plywood sheathing

they apply only to the housing sector.

Within the range of conventional construction techniques normally applied to single family housing, the *EBC* report evaluated a number of wall construction systems on the basis of a 1 square foot sample. Brick veneer on wood frame, for example, was shown to consume 126,426 Btu of embodied energy per square foot, as broken down in Table 14.

Of far lower energy intensity than this was an assembly using wood shingles on a wood frame, adding up to only 30,663 Btu all told; see Table 15. In a typical single family house the area of wall constructed in this way would amount to about 8 percent of the total energy consumed in construction and just over 10 percent of the embodied energy.

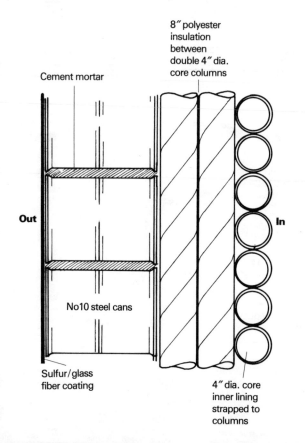

Cement mortar

8″ polyester insulation between double 4″ dia. core columns

Out

In

No10 steel cans

Sulfur/glass fiber coating

4″ dia. core inner lining strapped to columns

Table 16. A. Energy Analysis of Steel Can Newsprint-Core Stud Wall

Source: EBC report

	Btu per Square Foot
No. 10 steel cans (2)	6,000
Cardboard newsprint core	26,000
Scrap steel strapping	1,650
Sulfur coating	1,600
Glass fiber	980
Cotton polyester insulation (8 in.)	13,500
Total	49,730

B. Energy Analysis of Aluminum Can Sandwich Wall

Source: Author's estimate using *EBC* report technique

34. Steel can/newsprint core frame wall.

	Btu per Square Foot
Aluminum beverage cans (18)	117,000
Styrofoam, rigid (2 in.)	25,715
Cement, sand mortar	3,000
Total	145,715

C. Energy Analysis of Tire Wall

	Btu per Square Foot
Tire	1,000,000
Steel strap	1,200
Monofilament fabric	1,562
Gypsum wallboard (½ in.)	5,297
Wood battens (1 in. by 2 in.)	750
Wood blocks	1,000
Total	1,009,809

By comparison, three experimental waste assemblies are shown in Table 16. At first glance a ranking of these results suggests that conventional construction methods have little to gain from waste utilization. Of the five alternatives examined here, the two most energy intensive are waste systems, and even the best performing waste system has the drawback of being more complex than either brick on wood frame or shingle. Here, however, it is important to examine the basis for comparison, for just as the disposition of negative and positive signs can alter the meaning of an equation, so can an adjustment of energy credits and energy debits radically alter the apparent energy efficiency of the assemblies compared here.

35. Aluminum can sandwich wall.

36. Steel-strapped tire wall with fabric outer skin.

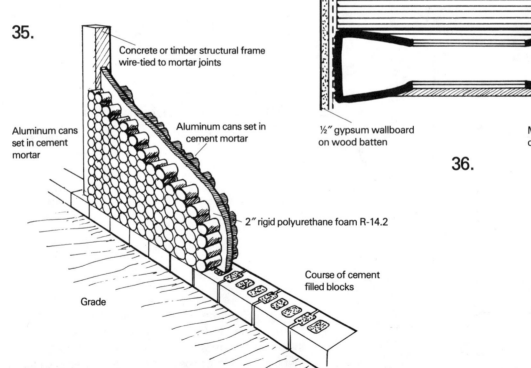

35.

Concrete or timber structural frame wire-tied to mortar joints

Aluminum cans set in cement mortar

Aluminum cans set in cement mortar

2″ rigid polyurethane foam R-14.2

Course of cement filled blocks

Grade

Vertical tensioning steel strapping

In

Tires

Out

½″ gypsum wallboard on wood batten

Monofilament fabric outer skin, painted

36.

Buildings As Energy Storage

Taking the tire wall as an example: its prime element, the auto tire, constitutes 99 percent of the embodied energy of the wall. This tire, if not used in a wall, would inevitably find its way into landfill or somewhere else in the environment where the 1 million Btu of petroleum used to make it would be lost.[5] At the stage of its life at which it is discarded, the tire possesses virtually all its structural strength and has lost only the thin layer of tread pattern that justifies its manufacture and sale as a transportation component. It is the performance of this thin layer, one-half of an inch at most, that covers the entire cost of producing the tire, distributing it, and rolling it to its final resting place. Tires employed in construction are, therefore, free of an embodied-energy cost as far as the construction sector is concerned, unless they are processed in some way before use in buildings. Furthermore, their retention in use effectively prolongs their life, for while any tire exposed to air and sun will eventually disintegrate through oxidation (if no other accident has destroyed it first), a tire buried in the wall or roof of a building will survive indefinitely.

Here, as in other cases, secondary use is synergetic: it is not only building but *energy storage*. It is as though the million Btu locked up in the tire were piled high in a warehouse, ready for recovery in ten, twenty, or fifty years time.[6] There is no better example of the value of storage in use than the use of tires in construction for the simple reason that no other waste product discarded in such quantity has so high an embodied-energy value.

From this standpoint, the energy intensity of waste materials is directly proportional to their value as energy savers through storage in use. Phosphate slime and copper tailings exist in enormous quantities, but their embodied-energy content is very low; to use them for building may be environmentally sound, but it cannot greatly alter the energy budget for any construction project. The 200 million tires abandoned every year, on the other hand, constitute 200 trillion Btu of embodied energy — a quantity equal to 3 percent of the energy used in the entire construction sector. The same is true of the 10 billion aluminum beverage cans, equal to 60 trillion Btu, or the 50 billion steel containers of all types whose combined embodied energy is as high as that of tires. Taken as a whole, the container and packaging industry dumps into the environment as much embodied energy as the construction industry consumes in the erection of single family housing every year. The total embodied energy of all reusable industrial, agricultural, commercial, and consumer wastes can only be guessed at: it must exceed the entire energy demand of the construction sector.

Seen in this light, the substitution of energy-intensive waste materials for conventional building assemblies offers not only the prospect of a reduction in the embodied-energy content of buildings, but also the conversion of these buildings into energy banks from which withdrawals may be made in the future. Thus the replacement of a shingled timber wall by a tire wall, while entirely justified on energy grounds, is not principally a building event — after all, only 10 percent of the embodied-energy budget for the house is involved. Much more importantly it represents a shift in the national energy budget, brought about by coupling the output and input of industries traditionally unconnected in any way. As with the example of the gasoline engine in Chapter 5 a small percentage increase in efficiency may not significantly alter operating economics, but an added use for the product can swing the energy balance in favor of net growth.

We shall return to this larger theme in due course, but it is possible to get some idea of its importance by applying the notion of an energy credit — the actual energetic value of the saving of waste from one industry by utilizing it in a second industry — to the comparisons made in the preceding tables. This will be done by introducing a second energy column representing the energy value of the waste employed and subtracting this from the embodied-energy content of the assembly itself to give a net energy intensity. The picture changes dramatically as a result.

In the calculation in Table 17 an energy credit has been applied for all wall components of waste origin on the assumption that construction use represents an alternative to loss. The role of the tire here is obvious, but some of the other components need a brief description. The steel strap is a section of scrap steel strapping reused with new seals to tension successive courses of the tire wall after completion. The monofilament fabric is a nylon textile made for the paper industry where it spends its short operational life in the form of a large (20 foot by 200 foot) belt used to dewater paper pulp; it is used here as an outer skin to the wall. The wood blocks, which are used to enable the tire to withstand vertical loads without deformation, are derived from mill off-cuts. All of these materials are waste and their storage in use represents an energy credit; the result is a wall assembly whose energy intensity is 95 percent lower than brick on wood frame and 80 percent lower even than shingle on wood frame. In practical terms this represents a reduction in the significance of the external wall as a component of the house: from 10 percent of all embodied

Source (Tables 17 and 18): Author's estimate using EBC report technique

Table 17. Revised Energy Analysis of Tire Wall

| | Btu per Square Foot | | |
Component	Embodied Energy	Energy Credit	Net Energy Intensity
Tire	1,000,000	1,000,000	
Steel strap	1,200	1,200	
Monofilament fabric	1,562	1,562	
Gypsum wallboard (½ in.)	5,297		5,297
Wood battens (1 in. by 2 in.)	750		750
Wood blocks (Ex. 2 in. by 4 in.)	1,000	1,000	
Totals	1,009,809	1,003,762	6,047

Table 18. Revised Energy Analysis of Steel Can Newsprint-Core Stud Wall

| | Btu per Square Foot | | |
Component	Embodied Energy	Energy Credit	Net Energy Intensity
No. 10 steel cans (2)	6,000	6,000	
Cardboard newsprint core	26,000	26,000	
Scrap steel strapping	1,650	1,650	
Sulfur coating	2,100	1,600*	500
Glass fiber	980		980
Cotton polyester (8 in.)	13,500	13,500	
Totals	50,230	48,750	1,480

*Allowance for process heat used in melting sulfur 500 Btu per square foot

energy, it now consumes less than 2 percent.

In the case of the steel can/newsprint-core stud wall (Table 18), the reduction in energy intensity is even more dramatic. By almost exclusively using waste materials, the saving over a brick on wood frame wall rises to 99 percent and for a shingle on wood frame to 95 percent. In effect, the embodied-energy content of the external walls of the house has ceased to be of any importance: a typical bathtub requires more energy to make than these walls. In a third example, shown in Table 19, the reduction is much less dramatic, but the result for a wall faced with aluminum on both sides is still less energy intensive than the most energy-efficient conventional system.

However impressive these results look, the absence of a labor cost component in both convention and waste assemblies should not be ignored. High labor costs might change the balance shown here, especially if the experimental assemblies proved difficult to simplify and refine. But if the labor question remains uncertain, there should be no confusion about the materials. The salvage items chosen for use as the basis for energy credits are bona fide wastes, all which exist in such quantities that construction demand — if such should develop — would not deform their price structure so as to remove the advantages examined here. Under present market conditions the construction industry as a whole consumes about 350,000 tons of extruded aluminum every year, as against 300,000 tons in packaging; 500 million square feet of single thickness window glass, as against 50 billion equivalent square feet in the form of bottles and jars; and 7,500,000 tons of steel, as against 7,000,000 tons used in cans and drums by the container industry. Even if all construction industry demand for these materials magically switched to container and packaging waste, the sector could all but hold the line.

The other important point to make at this stage is that the energy savings indicated here are achievable solely because the waste materials employed are used exactly as they are, with little or no energy expended on modification or preparation. This is the vital distinction between secondary use and recycling or reprocessing. If waste materials such as tires, bottles, or cans are retrieved from the waste stream and reprocessed into synthetic rubber, window glass, or steel and aluminum building components, then the additional energy inputs annihilate many practical advantages, as Table 20 shows.

Table 19. Revised Energy Analysis of Aluminum Can Sandwich Wall

| Component | Btu per Square Foot | | |
	Embodied Energy	Energy Credit	Net Energy Intensity
Aluminum cans (12 oz.)	117,000	117,000	
Styrofoam, rigid (2 in.)	25,715		25,715
Cement, sand mortar	3,000		3,000
Totals	145,715	117,000	28,715

Table 20. Energy Analysis of Reynolds Recycled Aluminum Wall System (1972)

| Component | Btu per Square Foot | | |
	Embodied Energy	Energy Credit	Net Energy Intensity
Aluminum siding	58,000	31,005*	27,495
Vapor barrier	—**		**
Plywood sheathing (½ in.)	5,779		5,779
Gypsum wallboard (½ in.)	5,297		5,297
Batt insulation (3½ in.)	6,860		6,860
Aluminum framing	156,000	82,680*	73,320
Totals	232,436	113,685	118,751

*Process energy required to convert cans into siding and framing assumed at 47 percent of virgin material processing cost (Hannon, 1972).
**Low, but not calculated

Source (Table 19 and 20): Author's estimate using EBC report technique

103

Here the resultant energy intensity, while reduced by half, is still considerably higher than any of the secondary use methods of building a comparable wall and only marginally lower than the most expensive of the two standard methods. General use of the Reynolds recycling technique, which was employed on a demonstration house project in Richmond, Virginia, in the 1972, would have no beneficial effect on the embodied-energy content of new single family houses.[7]

Although these comparisons have been confined to one element in the construction of single family housing, they strongly suggest that the use of energy-intensive wastes in construction should be further explored. If the concept of an energy credit resulting from storage in use is applied to the basic *EBC* embodied-energy analysis, all the waste techniques examined look more effective than recent recycling programs carried out within the container and packaging industries. The *EBC* report itself claims that the substitution of wood shingles for brick facing on all new single family houses would save the equivalent of 6 million barrels of oil a year. By the same token, the substitution of steel cans on newsprint cores for brick facing would save the equivalent of 8 million barrels.

As the next chapter will show, the secondary use of waste materials does not stop with one square foot of wall; nor is it confined to the more common consumer wastes. The techniques developed so far are primitive

37. Aluminum frame wall system, as used in the Reynolds Metals house, Richmond, Virginia.

compared with what might be achieved with one hundredth of the resources that have been plowed into other branches of energy research. Whether or not this approach could eventually have the kind of energy impact outlined in Chapter 5 as the possible product of a Keynesian energy policy is a matter for further investigation. What is already apparent is that energy-intensive wastes, if applied to the new construction of single family houses, could almost certainly reduce their embodied-energy content by 30 percent, a breakthrough that would make possible a proportional reduction in operating costs without a construction cost penalty.

Notes

1. An excellent interim summary of developments in this field is contained in United Nations Publication ST/ESA/51, *Use of Agricultural and Industrial Wastes in Low-Cost Construction* (New York: Center for Housing, Building, and Planning, Department of Economic and Social Affairs, 1976).
2. According to Gary Farmer, *Unready Kilowatts: The High-Tension Politics of Ecology* (Open Court, 1975), the only answer to waste and pollution is the expenditure of enormous amounts of energy to clear it up and dispose of it. Environmental controls are, he says, "an uncontrollable inflationary force," whose cost equals and often exceeds annual corporate profits in offending industries. He quotes the electricity consumption of an aluminum recycling plant for a city of 200,000 inhabitants at 10,000,000 kilowatt hours a year.
3. The Glass Container Corporation of Fullerton, California, which sponsored trials of "Envirite" and "Glasphalt," tried to persuade the architects of the Union Pacific bank built in downtown Los Angeles in 1974 to use a cladding material incorporating crushed waste glass. Although the terms offered were advantageous and the G.C.C. itself had sizable deposits with the bank, the architects refused, even though they admitted that aesthetically the waste-derived block was as good if not better than the costly finish finally chosen.

4. The argument that increasing conventional energy prices will soon make alternative energy economical embodies a dangerous flaw. First, the rate of increase in energy prices to consumers is uneven geographically and in relation to different fuels. Between 1972 and 1980 oil increased in price by 1,800 percent on the spot market but only by 350 percent on the domestic U.S. market. Over the same period natural gas prices rose only 150 percent, coal only 120 percent, and electricity by barely 100 percent (less than the price increase recorded by most consumer goods over the same period). This argues that the real rate of increase is much less in aggregate than is generally believed. Furthermore, even if energy prices do rise to meet the cost of photovoltaic generation, this will simply mean that there is no longer any cheap way to produce electricity, a fact which will have social and political implications far more serious than the opportunities for alternative energy it will create.
5. Of the 200 million tires discarded every year, fewer than 15 percent are recapped and less than 1 percent are reprocessed, burned in special furnaces, converted into fish reefs, or cut up to make industrial mats or boat bumpers. Despite the very large number of alternative uses for waste tires that have been canvassed in recent years, almost all of them eventually end up in landfill where they are notorious for the complications they create by resurfacing periodically.
6. Lest anyone should doubt the feasibility of just such an approach, *Time* magazine (23 May 1977) ran a story about Cecil Heidelberger of Andover, Minn., who collected between 8 and 10 million waste auto tires at his 10 acre ranch and trading post. In 1977 an Oklahoma salvage expert negotiated to buy the tires for $9 million with the intention of setting up a shredder on the ranch to process them into a saleable fuel additive.
7. The Reynolds Metals Company's "Recycled Home" is described in the next chapter. The energy analysis above was based on typical figures for the materials in question and not on information supplied by the Reynolds Metals Company; its accuracy is sufficient for the purpose of comparison only.

7 Early Experiments in Secondary Use Construction

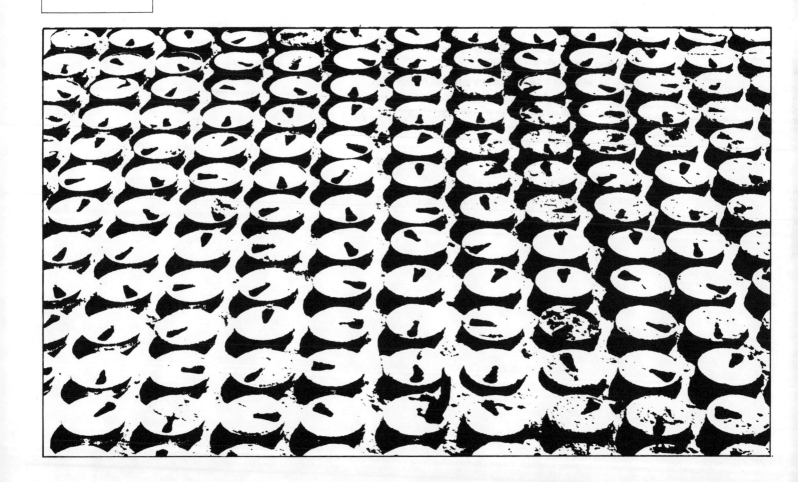

“ The recycled house dramatically demonstrates two points: first, that there are vast new markets for recycled materials if we just look for them. And second, even in sensitive areas such as residential housing, recycled products can look as good and behave as well as products made from virgin sources. As we began this project we decided that, in looks, it should not be distinguishable from other well designed, well built homes in the neighborhood. **”**

David P. Reynolds, "Recycled House,"
news conference, Richmond, Va., August 23, 1973

Early Experiments in Secondary Use Construction

Well, maybe. The fact that the Reynolds Metals house in Richmond, Virginia, looked like a conventional house and cost as much as one is undoubtedly important. In a sense it was a modern product of the mentality that made the first railroad cars look like stage coaches and the first airplanes look like kites. Recreation of the original regardless of cost is what separates recycling from secondary use.

Recycling occurs when old products are turned back into raw materials. Its chief drawback is that the energy that went into giving the bottle its distinctive shape or the can its remarkable dimensional tolerances is lost forever. Under recycling programs all cans are crushed, all bottles smashed, all tires shredded, all paper pulped, all plastic burned, and all structural strength, however great, remorselessly overwhelmed. In contrast, under secondary use the 10,000-pound crushing strength of the bottle (much higher than that of a brick or concrete block), the enormous tensile strength of the tire, the immense durability of the aluminum can, and the formability of the sulfur are all exploited to the utmost. In secondary use, old products are given a new life without being murdered first.

In fact, this is a very old idea, much older than recycling. Even the great architecture of the past shows some affinity with it, as, for example, the dome of San Vitale in Ravenna, Italy, which was constructed from converging circles of clay bottles 1,500 years ago. Whether the bottles were purpose-made or simply taken from stock for the job is less important than the fact that their remarkable lightness and strength were appreciated by ancient builders. Vernacular architecture too has always made use of salvage, incorporating fragments of older buildings — stones, timbers, windows, and so on. The most total use of this technique has come to be called by the French word *bricolage*, meaning odd-jobbery or the work of an odd-job man.

Although a tradition of *bricolage* in America has remained strong since frontier days, its most famous outburst was quite recent, taking the form of settlements built by counterculture communities during the 1960s. Various chance encounters persuaded the hippies to build domes instead of conventional structures, but good solid economics led them to use car tops, scrap timber, and demolition waste. The counterculture *bricoleurs* were deeply ambiguous in their attitude toward consumer technology and congenitally opposed to any large-scale building program. Every dome was a one-off dome, built the hard way with lavish hand labor and decoration, and this is one of the inherent problems with *bricolage:* it is not generalizable in the sense that it cannot be mass-produced or uniformly distributed.[1] There are thousands of examples of ingenious *bricolage,* and every one is different. From this point of view of building with waste, that is their limitation.

In developing countries the technique of *bricolage* is systematized to its highest level because it is how *most* building in such countries is done. In Latin America, Africa, India, and Southeast Asia it is a way of life, with a vast black market in waste or surplus materials feeding into it from a much smaller formal economy of consumption similar to that found in the West. Because of the enormous demand for materials and the limited supply (per capita consumption of canned or bottled beverages in the United States is 360 a year; in Chile it is 27), the technique of the Third World garbage builder is constrained by scarcity. Seldom does he have more than a handful of the same sized can, drum, bottle, or packing crate to work with. As a result, his building technology is opportunist and inconsistent, with none of the regularity and precision taken for granted in developed countries. If he could get 183,000 identical aluminum beverage cans (the number melted down to build the Reynolds Metals house), he would undoubtedly develop a more sophisticated product — especially if he could also obtain the cement necessary to bond them — but he is bound by the economics of his situation, and they militate against delay and material redundancy of any kind.

We in the West face a different problem and a different opportunity. For us it is not a question of finding more waste material in order to build more and better; it is a question of having too much energy-intensive waste

38. The famous Drop City domes of 1965, showing the virtues and limitations of *bricolage.* As regards richness of architectural expression, the contrast between this — the secondary use of car tops — and the conventionalities of recycling (**Fig. 45**) is instructive.

and nothing valuable to do with it. For us forty cans of different sizes, three tires, some wood and a torn sheet of polyethylene represent a disposal problem, not a basis for building. We can get 183,000 identical 12-ounce cans, 183,000,000 if necessary; a phone call brings a truckload of tires; a supermarket gives away a dumpster of cardboard. Bottles? How many do you need? Because of this difference, we in the West must concern ourselves with the development of large scale, high-performance building technologies based on our plentiful supply of energy-intensive wastes. We are not in the shelter business so much as the storage business. Building is a good way for us to store resources for the future.

It is for this reason that the magnificent products of

40.

39, 40, and 41. The tens-integral tower of pre-tensioned beer cans (**39,** shown here on its side, prior to erection) by Morris Schopf; and the chair assembled from a tire inner tube and steel strapping by Sterling King (**40**). The British advertising campaign for paint (**41**) takes the whole concept even further, but alas only in mock-up.

39.

41.

bricolage in the poorer quarters of the world are both an example of what can be done with waste and a warning of the quantifiable difference in situation between the energy rich and the energy poor. Third World waste builders have proved that there is no cheaper way to build than with that which is produced in massive quantity, whatever it is, from beer bottles to oil drums; but they and we face different issues, and the emulation of their labor-intensive *bricolage* does not optimize our own approach to garbage building.

The same kind of question mark hangs over the various art objects that have from time to time been created on the basis of secondary use. Ever since the "found objects" of the avant-garde in the 1920s, mass-produced, short-life products have figured in interior design, painting, and sculpture. As early as 1917 the Berlin apartment of "The Red Baron" — Manfred von Richthofen — was equipped with a pendant light fitting made from a radial airplane engine. Sometimes what is *bricolage* in origin becomes reclassified as art, as with the famous towers built by Simon Rodilla in the Watts neighborhood of Los Angeles. Sometimes the artistic creation matches or even excels what might have been done on a production line, as with the tensintegral tower of pretensioned beer cans, built by Morris Schopf at the University of Nebraska in 1972; or the chair assembled from a tire inner tube and steel strapping by Sterling King.[2] Graphic artists in advertising agencies deal conceptually with the idea of secondary use: the paint can that becomes a house or the breakfast cereal as a building block.

At the time of writing, all such artistic tendencies feed into a kind of secondary use chic called "high tech." The ingenuity it displays, in the form of a famous architect's tractor-tire furnished vacation home or a library shelved with industrial racking, is no more generalizable than that quintessential example of Third World *bricolage* — the Jamaican roadside store with uncut, milk-carton siding — not because such ideas cannot be repeated (they can and are) but because their value in the eyes of their originators is based on an imagined uniqueness which, if compromised, causes the inventor to look elsewhere.

Primitive or slick, touching or gross, the products of *bricolage* and art actually obscure the real economic and energetic significance of secondary use as a building principle. There is an irony in our romantic attachment to *barriadas* (squatter settlements) that is present also in our cultural output of side tables made from compressed off-grade cans or surplus magnesium racing wheels, our chromed Coca-Cola bottles and beer can cigarette lighters. Like Hero's *Aeleopile*, an ancient Greek precursor of the steam turbine, these toys amuse us year after year when really they should be put to serious work.

Apart from *bricolage* and art there are other phenomena related to secondary use in building — for example, the adaptive tradition within industry and engineering whereby one successful product is adapted to serve a variety of purposes instead of starting from scratch every time. Undoubtedly the most impressive example of this in recent years was the use by NASA of a Saturn Stage III booster module as the enclosure for the Skylab orbiting observatory, a perfect analogy for the Third World conversion of beverage cans into drinking mugs.

Another category of precursor is represented by the very small number of modern products that already are manufactured to serve multiple or successive functions. Perhaps the most impressive of these is the tank-tire, a combined wheel and fuel tank developed for military purposes but now used by oil companies and other prospectors in desert regions. The tank-tire is towable and can be maneuvered easily by one or two men so that the 50 gallons of gasoline it contains under air pressure can be used to refuel a stranded vehicle by opening the tire valve and allowing the liquid to flow through an attached hose inserted into the empty gas tank. Whether tank tires could be developed to become the fuel tanks of vehicles themselves, just as the double bottoms of ships became their fuel tanks when oil replaced coal, remains to be seen; but the possibility is there and the synergetic advantage evident.

As far as the future of the building industry is concerned, the dividing line between *bricolage,* artistic creation, and production ingenuity, on the one hand, and a genuine development of secondary use, on the other, is

easy to draw at a theoretical level, provided four basic principles are established.

1. *The use of waste products should, as far as possible, take place without preliminary energy-consuming industrial processing.* That is to say, building with bottles makes more sense than smashing bottles, color-sorting the glass and melting it down, and making special glass building components from it.

2. *The building technology developed to do this should adapt to the nature of the waste rather than try to make it conform to conventional construction techniques.* This means that if, for example, a way is sought to build with car components, then that way should be derived from

42. A Jamaican roadside store with uncut, milk-carton siding.

43. The Saturn Stage III booster, the casing of which was used as the framework for the Skylab orbiting observatory. An inspired high-technology example of *bricolage*.

the logic of automobile assembly and not from the traditions of building construction. Similarly, if the waste chosen were tires, then the result should exploit the resilience and tensile resistance of the tire.

3. *Specific building technologies should be developed to utilize all high-volume, energy-intensive wastes wherever output justifies the step,* that is, everywhere the volume of waste generated is equal to or larger than the volume of comparable building materials required for construction.

4. *If alterations to waste products or materials appear necessary in order to fit them better for their construction use, then these alterations should be introduced at the design stage prior to first use, not at the processing stage prior to secondary use.* This means simply that where efficient building is hindered by some factor determined by the design of the waste product or the physical properties of the waste material, then design should be the recourse rather than processing.

These four principles should be borne in mind in connection with the experimental secondary use buildings and projects now to be described.

44. Tank tires parked in the Saudi Arabian desert.

Processed Waste Buildings

Despite its nonconformity with the first principle of secondary use, the processing of waste products into building materials is the most common — one might say conventional — means of using waste in building. As examples mentioned earlier have shown, it is entirely feasible to convert wastes as disparate as animal dung and broken glass into building blocks, just as it is relatively easy to use waste rock or mine tailings in place of many types of aggregate. According to their promoters, "Envirite" and "Glasphalt" were both as good as and cheaper than existing products based on virgin materials. The Environmental Protection Agency too, in a report and supplement published in 1978 on the feasibility of using solid wastes for building materials, concluded that several basic agricultural wastes including rice hulls could be used to produce structural boards, synthetic sheetrock, a lumber substitute, and patented fire doors, all of which would be competitive with commercial products.[3] Four years earlier the Dutch Architect's Research Institute (SAR) in Eindhoven completed a four-part report arguing that waste cardboard could be used for furniture, partitioning, and even bathroom fittings in low-cost housing projects.[4] However, in none of these cases was an effort made to produce a complete building out of such materials, even though earlier experiments with plastics had more than once taken the form of a "house of the future." In fact, the Reynolds Metals house of 1972 represents the only example to date of a complete building assembled from waste products *processed* into building materials.

A partial estimate of the energy performance of the Reynolds Metals house has already been given in Table 20, but it is appropriate now to describe the project in more detail. The dwelling was conventional in appearance but incorporated virtually every known direct and indirect recycling process in the manufacture of the materials of which it was made. Four and one-half tons of 12-ounce aluminum beer and beverage cans were collected from recycling centers and transformed into aluminum ingots before being rolled and extruded into frames, joists, trusses, windows, rain water goods, and siding for the house. Twelve tons of crushed glass bottles were used as supplementary aggregate in the production of bricks and concrete blocks and directly in the driveway. Eight and one-half tons of newspaper were shredded and compressed into sheet and panel materials for sheathing, lining, and roof decking. Shredded tires provided a further additive for the driveway and steel mill slag was used in the insulation. All carpets in the house were made from reclaimed nylon fiber, and the carpet pads were made from old jute sacks. A floor tile was developed from scrap vinyl plastic, wood chips, and aluminum. Fly ash, collected in air pollution control equipment, replaced part of the Portland cement used in the concrete. Even the lawn contained compost processed out of New York garbage.[5]

At the time, the virtues of recycling were held to be self-evident, so the company did not publish any cost figures for the exercise. Nor could the $60,750 price tag for the house offer any guide as it was based on neigh-

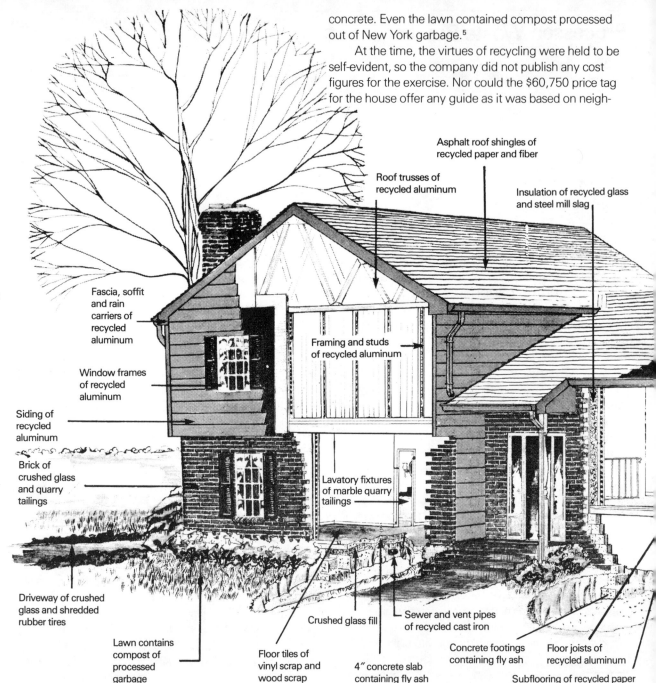

45. A cutaway drawing of the Reynolds Metals house, showing locations and types of waste materials used.

Asphalt roof shingles of recycled paper and fiber

Roof trusses of recycled aluminum

Insulation of recycled glass and steel mill slag

Fascia, soffit and rain carriers of recycled aluminum

Framing and studs of recycled aluminum

Window frames of recycled aluminum

Siding of recycled aluminum

Brick of crushed glass and quarry tailings

Lavatory fixtures of marble quarry tailings

Driveway of crushed glass and shredded rubber tires

Lawn contains compost of processed garbage

Floor tiles of vinyl scrap and wood scrap

Crushed glass fill

4" concrete slab containing fly ash

Sewer and vent pipes of recycled cast iron

Concrete footings containing fly ash

Floor joists of recycled aluminum

Subflooring of recycled paper

boring property values. A full-energy audit for the recycling procedures and the construction process would probably show that the Reynolds house was one of the most energy-intensive residential structures ever built in the United States.

At about the same time as the Reynolds house in

Virginia was nearing completion, work was just beginning on another experimental dwelling built with processed waste materials, this time on the outskirts of Montreal, Canada. This structure was much smaller and simpler than the Reynolds Metals house, and its use of wastes was less elaborate. Called the Ecol house, it was

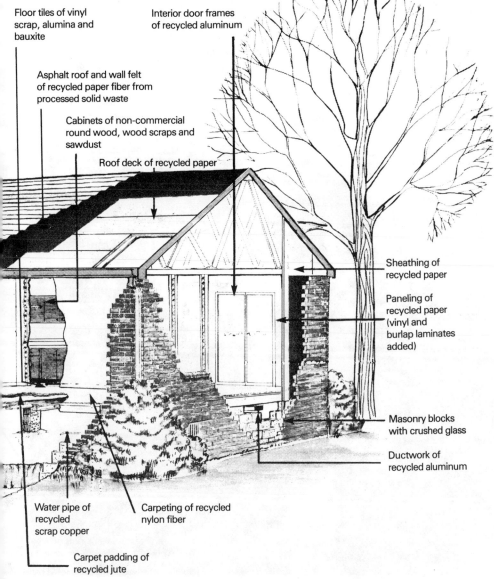

Floor tiles of vinyl scrap, alumina and bauxite

Interior door frames of recycled aluminum

Asphalt roof and wall felt of recycled paper fiber from processed solid waste

Cabinets of non-commercial round wood, wood scraps and sawdust

Roof deck of recycled paper

Sheathing of recycled paper

Paneling of recycled paper (vinyl and burlap laminates added)

Masonry blocks with crushed glass

Ductwork of recycled aluminum

Water pipe of recycled scrap copper

Carpeting of recycled nylon fiber

Carpet padding of recycled jute

117

built by the Minimum Cost Housing Group, a graduate program in the School of Architecture at McGill University headed by Alvaro Ortega and Witold Rybczynski, the latter of whom worked on the Dora Crouch house described in Chapter 1.

The Ecol house embodied a large number of alternative technology experiments, some more successful than others. It was intended originally to produce its own water by solar distillation, recycle its waste water, turn its solid waste into compost, provide for solar cooking and wind-generated electricity, and experiment with various economical means of construction. In the last case, its most revolutionary departure was the construction of a 144-square-foot room in sulfur concrete blocks that were cast in interlocking and self-aligning form in aluminum molds. A second secondary use feature was the scoring and splitting of large-diameter asbestos sewer pipes to form a self-supporting tile roof.

The sulfur technology developed here was extremely impressive and has since been refined and adapted in the Philippines and in Dubai. It has three main advantages over conventional concrete made with Portland cement: first, its status as a waste material, extracted in large quantities from pollution control equipment and petroleum refineries; second, its high strength and rapid setting properties (up to 7,000 pounds psi in compression with mold removal in fifteen minutes and complete curing in one hour); and, third, its low-energy consump-

46. The Ecol house of 1972. The sulfur block section can be seen to the left behind the solar cooker. The asbestos sewer pipe roof tiles are also visible.
pp153

tion—only 100,000 Btu per ton as opposed to 10 million Btu per ton for concrete. These advantages are, in the present state of the art, offset by brittleness and shrinkage (making large, complex molding difficult) and combustibility accompanied by the emission of toxic gas. It is anticipated that current development will overcome these problems and permit the absorption of a large part of the excess sulfur generated by pollution controls into construction and civil engineering projects. As long ago as 1944 the U.S. Institute of Paper Chemistry produced an experimental sulfur-impregnated paperboard house that stood for eight years. The Ecol and other simple dwellings designed for tropical and subtropical climates have since demonstrated that high-quality, high-strength, low-

47. Various types of sulfur concrete block developed at McGill. The design in back is based on a Peruvian model. The block in the right foreground was subsequently used in the construction of the Ecol house.

48. The largest structure built in sulfur concrete so far is the six-bedroom Maison Lessard in rural Quebec, which was completed in 1975. The external walls are made from cavity-filled sulfur blocks, laid dry and surface-bonded.

cost building is possible using sulfur blockwork. In *Maison Lessard* (see Figure 48), built with solid, internally insulated sulfur block walls in 1975, the Minimum Cost Housing Group applied the same technique in Canada with due regard for the rigors of the climate.[6]

Since building with stack-effluent sulfur is literally building with pollution (as Rybczynski claimed as long ago as 1972), its ultimate energy saving is net of the additional cost of the pollution control equipment. It is the high performance of sulfur concrete — or more correctly the high added value that sulfur concrete offers over waste sulfur at the price of heat and a quantity of sand — that justifies the processing applied to it. A ton of sulfur concrete can be mixed for the same energy input as is required to make fifteen aluminum cans or convert thirty into siding or extrusion, and one ton will produce more than 200 square feet of wall. In addition, there are different ways in which the basic substance can be used, depending on density and type of aggregate. Many materials including wood and cardboard can be impregnated with sulfur so that they are rigid or waterproof; others can be coated or sealed with it. As a basic binding agent, sulfur has an immense number of possible applications, in virtually all of which it would offer major energy savings.

Gernot Minke, director of the Research Laboratory of Experimental Building at the Technical University of Kassel, West Germany, has experimented in different directions with sulfur. He has developed a circular slip-form pouring technique capable of taking advantage of the extremely short setting time of the sulfur without using an inordinate number of molds, with the result that structurally monolithic sulfur shells can be built. He has also produced large sheet structural elements based on a buried fabric formwork for tensile strength, with insulation provided in the form of clay granules bonded to the panel with sulfur.[7]

The growing number of federally financed and private reports and surveys of waste material potential published in recent years strongly suggests that the production of building components from various processed wastes will increase in the future. Although this tendency is, of course, to be welcomed, it should be recognized that the energy expended on processing wastes is a debit, which, in circumstances that easily arise, can annihilate the economic advantage of using the waste at all. Using the neutral language of energy gain and loss is vital in assessing the true value of these methods. It is not sufficient to assign a disposal or "nuisance" cost and then subtract it from the cost of producing the surrogate material in order to arrive at a "market" price. In energetic terms, disposal is an option not a necessity.

49 and 50. Two experimental sulfur structures built at the Technical University of Kassel, West Germany. The monolithic sulfur concrete shell structure (**49**) was built using a rotary slip mold of diminishing diameter. The panel structure (**50**) used a buried fabric formwork for reinforcement and was insulated with clay granules bonded to the panel with sulfur.

True Secondary Use Buildings

In Chile during the economic siege of the Allende presidency, an immediate consequence was the unavailability of spare parts for foreign-made trucks and automobiles. Because of the geographical shape of the country, it is entirely dependent on road and rail transport for the operations of its economy, so the result was a desperate cannibalization of some vehicles to keep others (principally trucks) in operation. Consequently, a large number of bus bodies lacking engine or transmission parts became available, and administrative ingenuity determined that they should be used as emergency school classrooms in the squatter settlements ringing the major cities. Although lacking adequate headroom, they served well for this purpose; with their seats removed and chalk boards installed, they could be easily towed to the settlements, arranged in rows, and jacked up onto blocks.

This simple but productive substitution is a perfect example of the advantages of secondary use. The bus bodies were not ideal classrooms, but they were adequate and cost nothing. The cost of a comparable school building program would have been insupportable. Furthermore, it would have been possible in theory to feed certain design changes found desirable in classroom use through to the design of the bus so that what was being built in the future would be part bus, part classroom. As with other examples of secondary use, a primitive solution disguises a very sophisticated set of possibilities.

In economic terms the bus bodies are costed to the transport sector of the economy, depreciated in that function, and then transferred to education as a capital good. This aspect of their performance too must be included in any assessment of their real value as classrooms.

It is a far cry from the adroit exploitation of unavoidably immobilized vehicles in Latin America to the less common examples of the same line of thought to be found in the West. There two fundamentals of civilized life — housing and education — were approached by way of secondary use. Here, as we have seen, it is a matter of *bricolage*, art, advertising, and student projects. In all these areas themes emerge from time to time that hint at the real potential of the method but seldom in the form of complete buildings. The paint company advertisement and the student "muffler dome" (see Figure 51) are typical of a tendency that has, as we shall see in the next chapter, only surfaced once in the real world of mass production.

In terms of true secondary use for building in the United States, there can be little doubt that Michael Reynolds, an architect-builder from Taos, New Mexico, is the most prolific and serious practitioner in the field. Starting in 1972 shortly after graduating from the University of Cincinnati, Reynolds built the first of a series of steel- and aluminum-can-walled houses with the aid of some funding from the Continental Can Company.

51. A "muffler dome" built by students at Oxford Polytechnic, England, in 1974, using discarded automobile exhaust pipes cut to length, flattened, and bolted together.

The Natelson house (see Figures 53-54) was circular in form, and its walls were built on a "can block" system developed by Reynolds. Can blocks consist of eight aluminum or steel cans, two rolled flat and the whole bound together with baling wire. The resultant light 8-inch by 5-inch by 4.5-inch building block was tested for compliance with building codes by the University of Cincinnati and approved for two-story work. After erection of the walls of blocks using cement mortar, both inner and outer surfaces are plastered to prevent corrosion and provide a smooth finish.

Shortly after completion of the can-block house, Reynolds developed a new system using aluminum cans horizontally, bases outward, on either side of a sheet of 2-inch rigid styrofoam — the assembly analyzed in Tables 16 and 19. Called the "waste frame," this method of construction avoided the time-consuming assembly of can blocks by hand and made plastering of the wall unnecessary since both inner and outer faces consisted of the unperforated bases of aluminum cans. An intermediate structure, the 1973 Shriver house, was built using this method but with bimetal cans, with the result that the outer face of the walls was plastered and the inner painted; but from the 1974 Gale house onward, waste frame construction was used successfully in a number of houses, often in conjunction with poured concrete framing or timber post-and-lintel construction.

In 1975 Reynolds began experimenting with water-

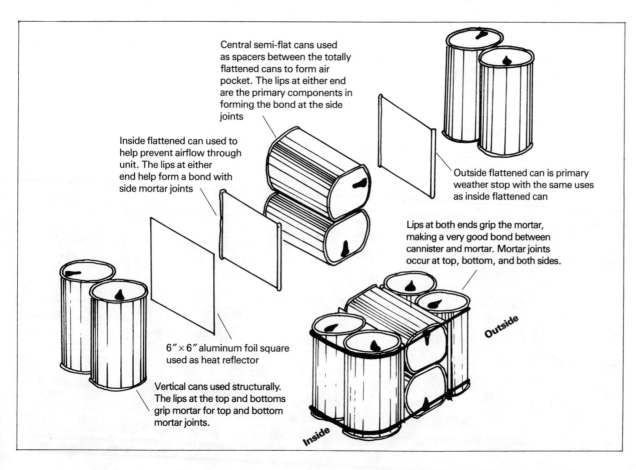

Central semi-flat cans used as spacers between the totally flattened cans to form air pocket. The lips at either end are the primary components in forming the bond at the side joints

Inside flattened can used to help prevent airflow through unit. The lips at either end help form a bond with side mortar joints

Outside flattened can is primary weather stop with the same uses as inside flattened can

Lips at both ends grip the mortar, making a very good bond between cannister and mortar. Mortar joints occur at top, bottom, and both sides.

6" × 6" aluminum foil square used as heat reflector

Vertical cans used structurally. The lips at the top and bottoms grip mortar for top and bottom mortar joints.

Outside

Inside

52. Drawing showing the components and construction of a "can block." The assembly of these blocks was carried out by itinerant labor prior to the construction of the Natelson house.

53. The Natelson house up to second-floor level, showing unplastered "can blocks" laid like bricks. Piles of unused blocks lie in the foreground.

54. The completed and plastered Natelson house in 1973. No cans are visible externally.

56.

57.

56 and 57. The Gale house under construction (56) and completed (57). The heavy poured-concrete frame enclosing the "waste frame" walls can be clearly seen. The final appearance of the house is marred by a small number of tin-free steel cans, which were undetected among the mass of aluminum ones used inside and out.

filled beverage cans as heat stores in passive solar housing. He purchased some can-closing equipment and unfilled cans from Continental and began with an electrical floor heating system using layers of water-filled cans beneath the floor of the waste-frame-constructed Curtis house. Although this installation was successful, local can suppliers refused to fill subsequent orders from Reynolds on the grounds that they were too small to be economical.

Another departure in 1975 was the first use of tires as a structural medium. Reynolds's first experiment was a small extension to his own home, which was built from tires filled with earth and stacked vertically rather than bonded or knit. This structure was partially underground in that the earth to fill the tires was taken from inside the walls. The columns of tires were themselves held together by a wooden bond beam at eaves level. Internally the interstices in the wall were patched with mortar and the whole surface painted.

A second small tire structure was designed by using a model made of Lifesaver candies, and was built in 1975. This time the tires were bonded like brickwork, and every third course was strapped together. Each tire was filled with earth and then individually leveled parallel and perpendicular. Then the entire wall was topped with a wooden bond beam, held in place by lengths of reinforcing bar set into a cement mortar filling to the top row of tires. As in the earlier structure, the resultant house was partially underground as the earth to fill the tires was taken from the interior, but in this case earth was bermed up against the outer walls as well. With the exception of the design improvement of stepping the wall tires down to grade level, which was introduced in 1977, and the use of expanded metal nailed to the inner surface of the tires and plastered, which was adopted in Reynolds's own 1978 tire house, this technique became standard for tire building in New Mexico. The 1978 example received a state building permit and was financed with a conventional bank building loan.

Michael Reynolds achieved another breakthrough in waste construction in 1976 when he discovered that it was possible to build domed structures without centering, using aluminum cans—an unconscious repeat of the San Vitale method that used clay bottles 1,500 years earlier. Reynolds's desert dome used a double layer of aluminum cans with an 8-inch insulated air space between them. Since the cans were so light that they would adhere to the wet mortar used to corbel in the dome, it was possible to close both skins at the center without any formwork. Can domes were used in the 1977 Sherer house, with the outer skin plastered to provide a leak-proof surface.

Reynolds's *oeuvre* in waste materials is more impressive than that of any other designer or builder. At the

58. The passive solar Curtis house in winter. Using a timber frame instead of the massive concrete structure of the Gale house, the Curtis house has electric under-floor heating using water-filled aluminum cans.

59.

time of writing, at least twelve houses in and around Taos have been built by him from cans, bottles, and tires, with their roof framing cut from dead trees found on the mesa. These structures, which have been financed, sold, and resold using conventional bank or savings and loan mortgages, prove beyond question that secondary use is feasible and socially acceptable, even bankable in the sense that its uniqueness enhances its value as real estate.

Reynolds has imparted his expertise to the United Nations, the Venezuelan government, and to various universities and has a vast collection of press cuttings and television news items from abroad as well as within the United States to show for his efforts. There is no doubt that the techniques he developed are simple and economical, if relatively labor intensive and given to idiosyncracy. Still, they tend to act as *starting points* for his imitators and disciples rather than techniques to be emulated. His work is both homespun and, somehow, anti-industrial. American architects tend to react against the former, Europeans against the latter. Both take away the example and try to better it, primarily (alas) in schools and universities. The fact that no one has emerged from this pursuit with a continuing practice or even a sequence of buildings to compare with Reynolds's is perhaps testimony to how far ahead he really is.[8]

When I first became aware of Reynolds's work, I was concerned with efforts to reduce the amount of

60.

59 and 60. Reynolds' first-ever tire structure (**59**) using unbermed earth-filled tires lashed together every third course and plastered on the outside. Later structures like the 1978 tire house used size-coordinated tires and external berming to improve stability (**60**). The inner surface of the tire wall is covered with expanded metal and plastered on completion.

61.

61 and 62. Virginia and Mike Reynolds building the 1976 desert dome without centering (**61**), and its completed appearance (**62**). The cement plastering was done to prevent leaks, as with the later Sherer house, which used the same dome structure.

62.

cement mortar consumed in can-laying by whatever means. One early experiment involved braizing cans together with a propane torch and filling only the interstices with mortar. Another, carried out by industrial designer Shiu Kay Kan, who works in London, involved spot welding the cans together in the same way. Later, Kan developed small plastic clips, but the final solution to the mortar problem was to precast panels of cans set in mortar, complete with reinforcement. This way their appearance could be regularized and the amount of mortar used cut to a minimum; furthermore, the method facilitated prefabricated assembly. Two years after experimenting along these lines at the Experimental Low Cost Construction Unit of Florida A&M University, I was shown examples of houses built in Tecate, Baja California, using this very method but with the can tops and bases plastered over.

Another Reynolds starting point was tires. Anyone who has taken part in or even observed tire building will perceive that it is very labor intensive. The tires *have* to be packed by hand and each one will take a wheelbarrow full of sand or earth. Their weight too is enormous, and maneuvering them wholly or partially filled is very difficult. At the same time, although earth-filled tires are in tension (like balloons filled with water), the tire wall itself does not use the enormous tensile strength of each tire as efficiently as if, for example, it was part of a net or web. Logically, therefore, or so it seemed at Florida

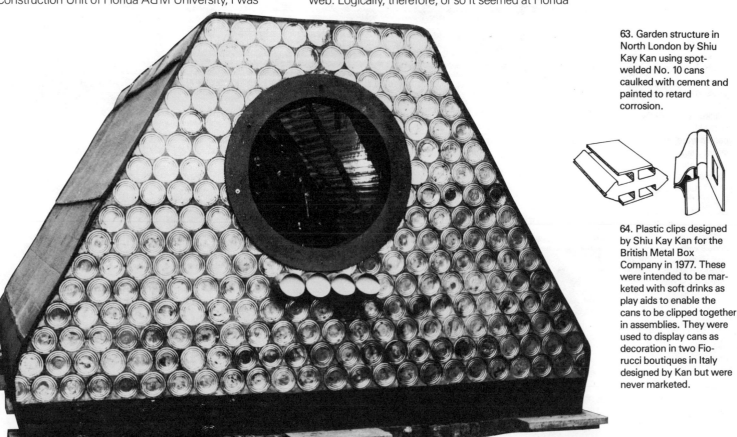

63. Garden structure in North London by Shiu Kay Kan using spot-welded No. 10 cans caulked with cement and painted to retard corrosion.

64. Plastic clips designed by Shiu Kay Kan for the British Metal Box Company in 1977. These were intended to be marketed with soft drinks as play aids to enable the cans to be clipped together in assemblies. They were used to display cans as decoration in two Fiorucci boutiques in Italy designed by Kan but were never marketed.

65.

66.

65, 66, and 67. Eight-foot by four-foot precast reinforced-concrete panels using aluminum beer cans exposed on both sides as voids for lightening. Designed by Millard Wright of Florida A&M University, these panels were used to construct a sign (**66**) surmounted by thinner concrete panels using wood chip aggregate. Each of the house panels used 377 aluminum cans and scrap steel strapping reinforcement. Similar panels with the cans flush-faced were later observed in use in Baja, California (**67**).

67.

A&M, we should try to build with tires in this way. Our earliest experiments with nets—joining the tires with scrap steel strapping—proved that considerable weights were involved here too. A strong central column, steel cable, pulley blocks, and a truck winch were necessary to erect the first examples, which were, nonetheless, strong and stable when in position. Pyramidal, conical, and ridged structures were built and, with difficulty, erected. At length, graduate student Alan Wolfe broke through this impasse by designing and building a simple tire-stripping machine that cut the tread from the tire and left two side walls, each of which had almost the tensile strength of the whole tire because the bead was undamaged. With this system, much lighter structures were

possible, and Wolfe himself developed one using the tread of the tire to fill the hole in the center so that the entire roof structure could be covered with earth or any other material capable of adapting to compound catenary curves.[9] Only later did we discover that Karl-Ernst Kerkhof of Bremerhaven, West Germany had already patented a roofing system using the treads alone, alternately up and down facing, nailed like shingles.[10]

Apart from net structures, the other solution to the tire weight problem was a much lighter wall. At first we tried to solve this by using a filling different from sand or earth; bottles were tried, then rings of beverage cans, and finally wood off-cuts from sawmills that would otherwise be burned. This last method worked well provided

68. Two tire-net roof structures erected at Florida A&M University. In the background, a ridge beam structure using bias-angled roofing sheets. In the foreground, a hexagonal roof with ring beam and central column. Although successful, the great weight of these structures led to the development of the tire-stripping technique to lighten the net.

131

Elevation

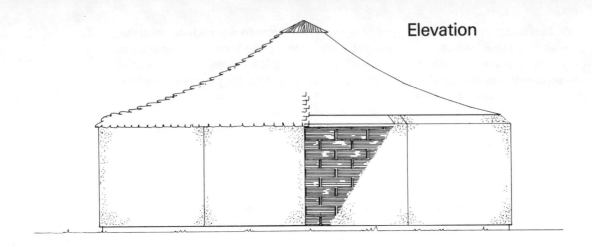

View in Cross Section

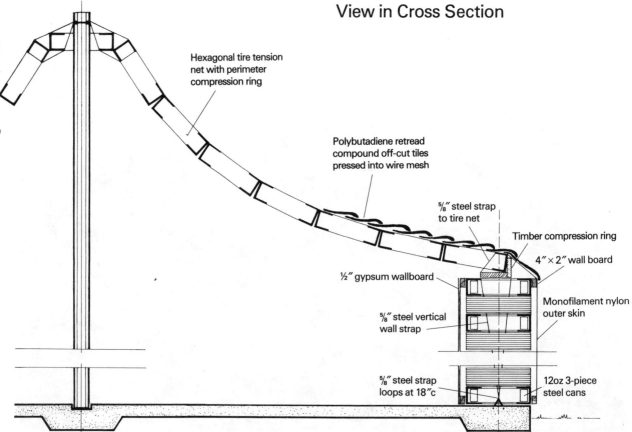

69. Views of design for a small tire house developed for presentation to the Jamaican ministry of housing. This structure was to have used a monofilament nylon outer skin (a paper mill waste) coupled with a tire-net roof and "tropical" tire walls. The roof tiles were derived from recap off-cuts, also a waste.

Hexagonal tire tension net with perimeter compression ring

Polybutadiene retread compound off-cut tiles pressed into wire mesh

⅝″ steel strap to tire net

Timber compression ring

4″ × 2″ wall board

½″ gypsum wallboard

Monofilament nylon outer skin

⅝″ steel vertical wall strap

⅝″ steel strap loops at 18″c

12oz 3-piece steel cans

132

the wall was tensioned down from eaves to slab with steel straps, the result being very quick to build and quite possible to surface internally with expanded metal and plaster or conventional sheetrock. The external surface was intended to be stretched monofilament nylon that was spray-painted to make it waterproof. This type of wall, with its large perforated inner core of tires, was ideal for convection air movement and for cooling as well as heating by the sun and, consequently, seemed suitable for a number of tropical or high-humidity locations where cheap housing was required. A complete small house design was worked out for this, and some interest was shown in Jamaica and Brazil.

In his early New Mexico work Michael Reynolds had frequently used bottles in construction, either bases inward to provide a multicolored translucent wall or water filled as part of a heat bank. Neither of these applications really exploited the enormous compressive strength of cylindrical glass structures, and it was left for Gernot Minke to explore these possibilities in West Germany. Not content with carrying out compression tests on individual bottles as we had at Rensselaer Polytechnic Institute,[11] he studied the load-carrying capacity of rings of bottles glued together and superimposed in the form of columns. To his amazement he discovered that a seven-bottle column of standard 12-ounce beer

Roofing and Eaves Detail

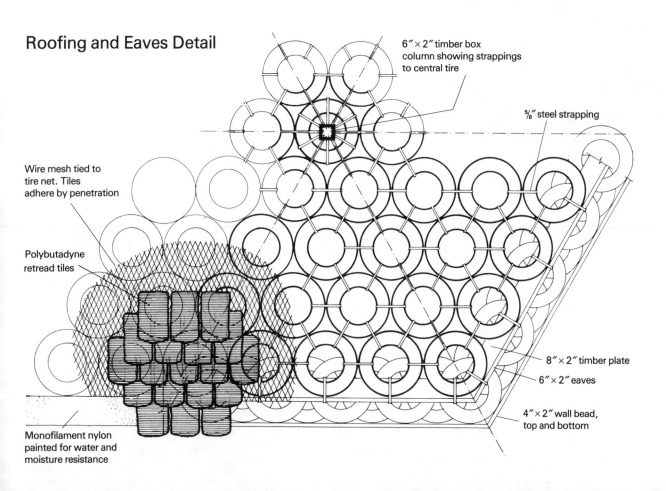

6″ × 2″ timber box column showing strappings to central tire

⅝″ steel strapping

Wire mesh tied to tire net. Tiles adhere by penetration

Polybutadyne retread tiles

8″ × 2″ timber plate

6″ × 2″ eaves

4″ × 2″ wall bead, top and bottom

Monofilament nylon painted for water and moisture resistance

133

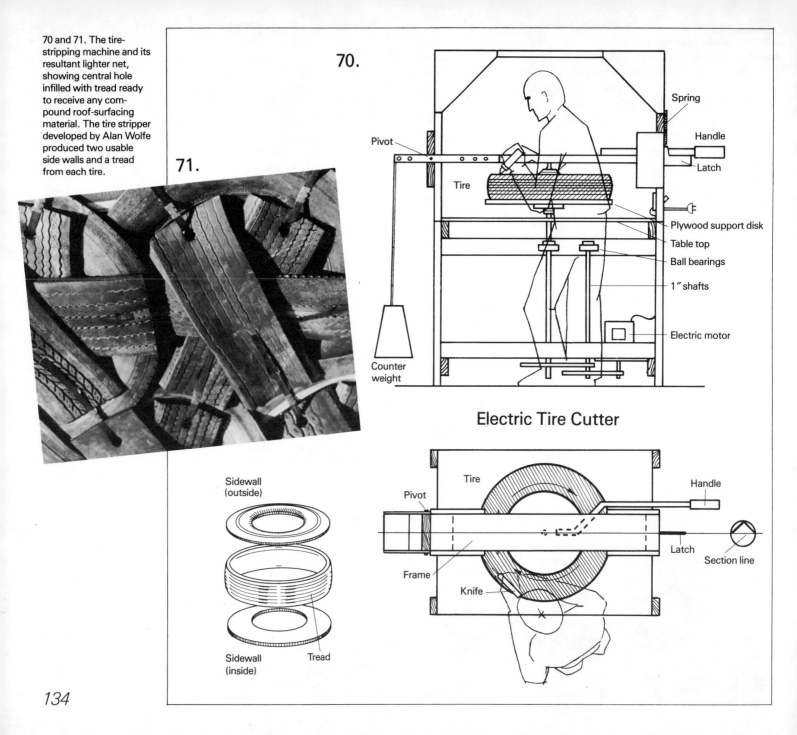

70 and 71. The tire-stripping machine and its resultant lighter net, showing central hole infilled with tread ready to receive any compound roof-surfacing material. The tire stripper developed by Alan Wolfe produced two usable side walls and a tread from each tire.

70.

Pivot

Spring

Handle

Latch

Tire

Plywood support disk

Table top

Ball bearings

1″ shafts

Electric motor

Counter weight

Electric Tire Cutter

Sidewall (outside)

Sidewall (inside)

Tread

Tire

Pivot

Frame

Knife

Handle

Latch

Section line

71.

72. The tread itself could be used as a roof covering, as shown here in the German-patented Kerkhof system.

73. The "tropical" tire wall developed at Florida A&M University in 1979. Using small wooden off-cuts as spacers, the empty tires were laid and tensioned into position using steel strapping. The outer skin was to have been formed from painted monofilament nylon and the inner from gypsum plasterboard on battens. Air movement up and down the tire honeycomb was to have been controlled by adjustable vents at top and bottom. Standing on the wall are graduate students Bill Kesterson, Blakeley Bruce, Millard Wright, and Ebby Mowlavi.

135

74. Kassel-tested bottle column capable of carrying 17,000 pounds vertical load without failure.

bottles would support a load of 8,800 pounds, a performance within the engineering or bridge-building range and far superior to the strengths required for one- or two-story housing. By reversing alternate courses of bottles so that bases met bases and necks met necks, he increased the vertical load to 17,600 pounds per column! These figures mean that nonreturn bottles, of which perhaps 25 billion are dumped or smashed every year, have a potential compressive strength almost as high as that of steel. If an appropriate building technique were developed to take care of shear and tensile stresses, bottles could be used to build skyscrapers!

Minke's own use of bottles in construction took the form of a small demonstration building completed in

75.

75 and 76. Test structure built by Gernot Minke and students at Kassel in 1977 (**75**) with bitumen-bonded bottle wall (left) and cardboard-clad walls reinforced with an inner filling of vertically stacked bottles. The roof structure (**76**) was formed in cardboard vaults reinforced with glued beverage cans, clerestory lit with more bottles after erection.

76.

77.

1977 in Kassel, in which the vertical columns of bottles supporting the roof were encased in waterproofed cardboard. The end wall of this structure was composed entirely of bottles glued together with bitumen rather than bonded in mortar in the more usual way, and the floor was formed from the bases of bottles with the interstices packed with cement. The roof was composed of a number of prefabricated vaulted structures using bimetal cans as spacers and waterproofed cardboard as an outer and inner surface. The use of bottles as vertical supports acted as an excellent counterbalance to the hydroscopic nature of the cardboard wall surfaces, which would otherwise have distorted under the roof load over time.

A series of experiments carried out by Minke at

78.

77 and 78. Leonard Koren's sandbag structure built at UCLA in 1973 (**77**) bore a striking resemblance to another Minke experiment carried out at Kassel. There 10-foot lengths of polyester fabric tube were filled with earth and laid in a self-supporting beehive structure in 1977.

Kassel that had no analogue in the work of Michael Reynolds involved the use of sand and earth without such binders as cement, lime, or resins. In the earliest of these structures, built in 1977, Minke and his students used a continuous tube of polyester fabric 1 foot in diameter cut into 10-foot lengths and filled with sand or earth by means of a specially designed air blower. The lengths of tube were superimposed in a reducing diameter beehive structure 10-feet high. Later versions of this technique applied to vertical walls used the same 10-foot sacks wound into coils around the timber frame and painted externally. The final version, used experimentally in an aid project in Guatemala in 1978, employed the sacks stretched out in lines and restrained by bamboo stakes inside and outside, connected by ties at intervals.

In this case too, the sacks were painted with lime for preservation. [12] All of these sand and earth building methods lend themselves to use with any dry granular waste.

Secondary use experiments of one kind or another have been made with most of the better-known, energy-intensive consumer and industrial wastes, and the results are sufficiently encouraging to suggest that organized building output by this means might be an alternative or supplement to recycling in urban areas. As their enormous strengths alone indicate, bottles and tires should be subjected to much more investigation: if the great compressive strength of the former could be allied to the tensile strength of the latter, some very ambitious low-embodied-energy structures might result.

79. As part of an aid mission project in Guatemala in 1978, Minke used the sandbag technique for low-cost housing with the sacks laid in lines, restrained with bamboo, and painted with lime for protection.

Preconsumer Wastes: Buildings from Someone Else's Production Line

In the 1930s and 1940s, the heyday of enthusiasm for prefabricated housing, it was confidently believed by the editors of *Fortune* and by the man in the street that in a very few years most houses would be built on production lines, run off and delivered like cars from competing dealerships. Except in the mobile home industry, which is responsible at best for 25 percent of the houses built in the United States, it never happened; yet the image of the automobile production line has haunted architects, builders, and others responsible for housing for most of the present century. The application of the idea of secondary use to this principle is as yet tentative and has nowhere achieved more than the status of a project, but it is nonetheless of interest.

There are two elements in the underlying theory: first, that the capital and development costs involved in mass-producing buildings using purpose-made components could be avoided by assembling them out of items that are already mass-produced in great quantity; and second, that within production processes there are always sufficient off-grade items generated to support a second use without diverting those good enough for their designated function. In practical terms this means, for example, that because the production of beverage cans or bottles in the United States is carried out on a scale ten times larger than that of bricks or concrete blocks, it might be cheaper to base building prefabrication on can or bottle technologies than upon scarcer and more expensive items such as purpose-made building materials. A corollary to this example is the additional possibility of diverting cans or bottles that fail on-line quality control tests from consumption to building, thus increasing even more the overall efficiency of the production process.[13]

My own thoughts along these lines were first triggered when I was in Chile at the invitation of the government Ministry of Planning (ODEPLAN), searching for ways to increase housing production without absorbing existing building labor and resources. I was intrigued by the spectacle of the reuse of bus bodies and the idea that they might one day be *designed* to serve as emergency classrooms as well as buses, with modifications built in on the production line. At the time (1972) it was characteristic of the country's economic siege that the Santiago plant of Citroen Chilena SA, producing small Citroen cars and vans from Belgium, should have been closed down because no more engines and transmissions were being imported. The native capacity to produce pressed metal body and chassis parts was thus rendered useless and was, indeed, at the time being attacked by the Allende government as an example of the poor organization of industry in the past.

80.

80 and 81. The Citroen
Chilena SA project of
1973. Using body parts
from the small Citroen
van manufactured in
Chile, it was possible to
design a metal housing
system for mass pro-
duction during the
shortage of imported
mechanical parts. The
project, carried to an
early design stage at
Cornell University,
was not developed.

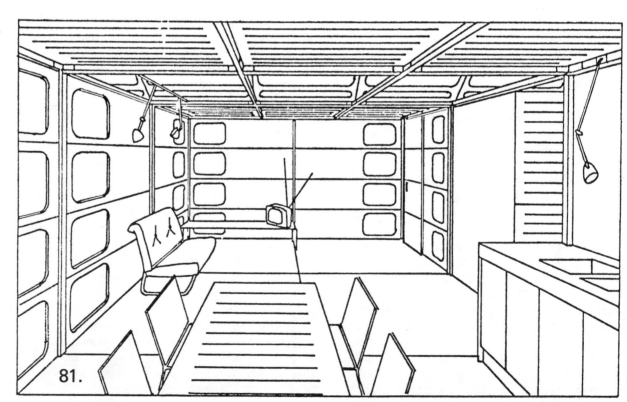

81.

It seemed to me that the strong similarity between the body parts of the 2CV (*Fourgonette*) van and those used to produce light industrial buildings in Europe might make some secondary use possible. With the acquiescence of ODEPLAN it was agreed that this matter should be looked into further, and the following year at Cornell University a preliminary design was produced showing how Santiago-made body parts could be assembled into emergency housing units. The disastrous coup of 1973 in Chile abruptly terminated this project along with many other advanced notions espoused by the *Unidad Popular* government, but not before it had become clear that the potential for house production by this means was considerable. In Chile annual housing output at that time reached 60,000 units. Based on pre-1970 vehicle production figures, Citroen Chilena SA ought to have been able to produce another 10,000 van-based emergency units a year.[14]

The example of the *Fourgonette* project led to the design of two similar buildings in the Netherlands a few years later, but neither one progressed beyond project stage. The designer in both cases was an architect named Rinus van den Berg, then of the Dutch Architect's Research Institute (SAR). Van den Berg worked first on the combined use of Volkswagen camper roofs, oil drums, and specially designed reusable Heineken bottles for a single-story office building. This project (see Figure 82), in comparison with any building by Michael Rey-

82, 83, 84 and 85. Two Dutch projects by Rinus van den Berg based on the Citroen example. Both the competition entry for an architectural research building (**82**), and the solar-heated ATIM project (**83** and **84**) used oil drum columns, WOBO (WOrld BOttle) walls (see **Figs. 91** and **92**), and van roof panels (continued on next page).

82. Design for the SARBURO Building

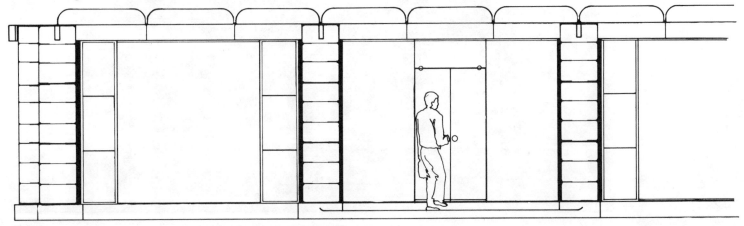

83. Solar-Heated ATIM Project

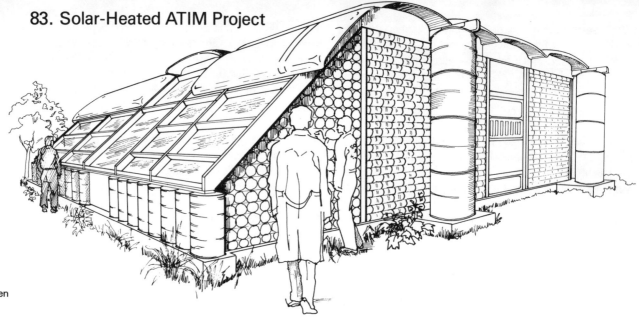

83, 84 and 85. In the SARBORO scheme, Volkswagen camper roofs were to have been used, in the ATIM design, Peugeot type J–6 (**85**). Neither of these projects went further than model stage despite initial financial backing from manufacturers.

84.

85.

nolds, shows the difference between European and American approaches to secondary use. Based on a square grid, van den Berg's office was designed around superimposed oil drum columns and glass bottle walls; the Volkswagen roof panels were to have been joined at their edges and corners by purpose-made plastic moldings.

While this project was never executed, it attracted considerable interest, and in 1975 Van den Berg began to put together a powerful consortium of industrial backers to fund a new building project on an appropriate scale. The first of these supporters was Alfred Heineken, whose unique contribution to secondary use design will be described in due course. Next came Phillips Electrical, of Eindhoven, Holland, like Heineken Breweries a multinational corporation of enormous wealth; Van Leer, a large-scale producer of containers such as oil drums; and, finally, Pon, the largest Volkswagen distributor in Holland. These four backers reached an agreement with the SAR, and work began on a pilot project designed to gently usher the consortium of brewers, electronics experts, container manufacturers, and car dealers into the construction business.

Unfortunately for the future of secondary use, the project itself rapidly became a football bounced from side to side by the interests of the participants. The title was changed twice, first to ATIM (an acronym based on the Dutch word for alternative use, *Toepassing*) and finally to ATIP (AlTernative application of Industrial Products). The Technical University of Eindhoven, which offered a site, later demanded a two-year monitoring exercise within the original budget. Moreover, all the participants felt strongly that the real experiments should be solar, with hydroponic gardens, rain water collection, and other complications. As a result of these pressures the design went through a succession of drastic revisions, culminating in a large and expensive architectural model that was lavishly illustrated in the Italian magazine *Domus* in the fall of 1976. In this final form the design called for various Volkswagen components including roofs and doors. As with the office building, the roof supports took the form of oil drum columns, and the translucent walls were made of Heineken bottles. The south wall of the house was conventionally glazed and sloped at an appropriate angle for the numerous solar experiments to be installed within. Before construction could begin, the consortium fell apart, the principal members withdrawing early in 1977. Since that time Rinus van den Berg has published one or two more secondary use designs, one involving the use of compressed car bodies for walls. He has also published articles in Holland on the economic implications of secondary use and multipurpose products.[15]

The only other project of this kind with which I am acquainted is the Chilean artist Matta's "*Autoapocalypse*," built between 1973 and 1976 in Italy and exhibited in 1978 in Florence. This structure, which takes the form of a house made almost entirely from Fiat 600 components, was intended by its creator as a commentary upon the isolation and alienation of modern man at the wheel of his automobile. This daunting symbolism notwithstanding, it is an impressive physical manifestation of secondary use, inhabitable as a house and—juxtaposed with other Fiat 600's crushed into bales—a fitting reminder of the as yet unexplored possibilities generated by the mass production success of the automobile.

In addition to buildings constructed from processed wastes, buildings resulting from true secondary use, and buildings based on the diversion of production line objects conceived for another purpose, there is a fourth category of waste building. This variation — *buildings assembled from components specially designed for secondary use* — is in many ways the most sophisticated and promising category of all, and for this reason it will receive its own chapter.

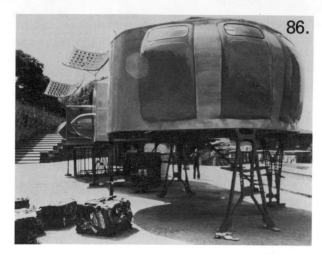

86.

86 and 87. Two views of the Chilean artist Matta's "Autoapocalypse," exhibited in Florence, Italy, in 1978. Designed entirely from Fiat 600 body and chassis parts (with some linking sheet metal sections), this structure unconsciously demonstrated many of the adaptive possibilities of secondary use. A later Fiat project, the TOTEM (Total Energy Module), using a 127 engine derated to run on natural gas as the power cell for a single-family house, was marketed two years later, showing that the company is possessed of a full genetic pool of adaptive ideas, even if few of them are used.

87.

Notes

1. The writings and constructions of the counterculture are enigmatic already, after an interval of only fifteen years. According to Peter Rabbit (*Drop City,* New York: Olympia Press, 1971), the decision to build domes at the settlement that gave his book its name was taken on the basis of chance attendance at a lecture by Richard Buckminster Fuller. Previously, A-frames had been intended. Although Rabbit stresses the cheapness and simplicity of dome building with car tops and urges the world to emulate the "droppers'" technique, he dwells for several pages on the hard labor and unpleasant injuries sustained by all who worked on these once famous buildings. The concept of the energy credit is enunciated in car top economics: 3½ ft. by 7 ft. sheets of 27-gauge steel with baked-on enamel paintwork for fifteen minutes work and 15 cents to the car dump owner (in 1965). Car tops were cheaper and better than plywood for dome construction; Drop City's domes were built for less than $20 each, most of that for sheet metal screws.

2. Illustrated in Dona Z. Meilach, *Creating Modern Furniture* (New York: Crown, 1975).

3. *The Feasibility of Utilizing Solid Wastes for Building Materials,* Report EPA-600/8-77-006 and Supplement EPA-600/2-78-111 (Washington, D.C.: Environmental Protection Agency, 1977 and 1978).

4. *Wonen met Karton* (Eindhoven, Netherlands: Stichting Architecten Research, 1974). The publication consists of an introduction and portfolios of design details covering partition walls and false ceilings, living room and bedroom furniture, and kitchen and bathroom fittings.

5. These details are taken from *The Home Recycling Built,* a press kit supplied by the Reynolds Metals Company to the author in 1974.

6. The account of the sulfur components of the Ecol house and the properties of sulfur is taken from articles by Witold Rybczynski: "The House That McGill Built," *Canadian Architect,* March 1974; and "Sulfur Building," *Architectural Design,* December 1975. In addition, there are numerous publications on the subject available from the Minimum Cost Housing Group.

7. Gernot Minke, "Alternative Construction Technologies and Materials for Low-Cost Housing," unpublished paper delivered to First International Conference of Garbage Architects (FICOGA), Tallahassee, Fla., May 1979.

8. This account of Michael Reynolds's construction methods is taken from a conversation with him on May 27, 1977; from "A Chronological Listing of Mike Reynolds Houses and Architectural Techniques in Taos, New Mexico," unpublished monograph by Alan Wolfe and Larry Birch (1978) of the Experimental Low-Cost Construction Unit, Florida A&M University; and from an unpublished paper delivered by Michael Reynolds to the First International Conference of Garbage Architects (FICOGA), Tallahassee, Fla., May 1979.

9. Alan Wolfe, *Tera: A Tire and Earth Roof Assembly,* unpublished master's thesis, Florida A&M University, 1979.

10. Karl-Ernst Kerkhof, "New tire-roof system demonstrated," photo caption in *Building Design* (London), 25 June 1976.

11. The Rensselaer Polytechnic tests, carried out by the author in 1976, used only single examples of different types of nonreturn bottle. The poorest vertical load performance recorded was 3,500 pounds for an 8-ounce mixer bottle: the best—11,000 pounds for a 48-ounce Coca-Cola "Crowd Pleaser."

12. Minke, *Alternative Construction Technologies.*

13. In a typical bimetal can production facility, between 1 and 2 percent of all cans produced are leakers (they fail a pressure test) and must be treated to remove the tin coating already applied to them before the metal of which they are made can be reused. Since can forming lines produce barrels at a rate of about 1,200 per minute, the quantity of leakers produced per day from a large plant can reach 100,000. If these cans were usable in construction whether or not they leaked, it would be more economical to build with them than to recycle them.

14. A more detailed account of this episode is contained in Martin Pawley, *Garbage Housing* (New York: Halsted, 1976).

15. These details are derived from conversations and correspondence with Rinus van den Berg from 1974 to 1979. His work has occasionally been illustrated in European magazines, notably *Domus* (Milan), Fall 1976, and *De Architect* (Amsterdam), March 1977.

Product Eugenics: Design for Evolution

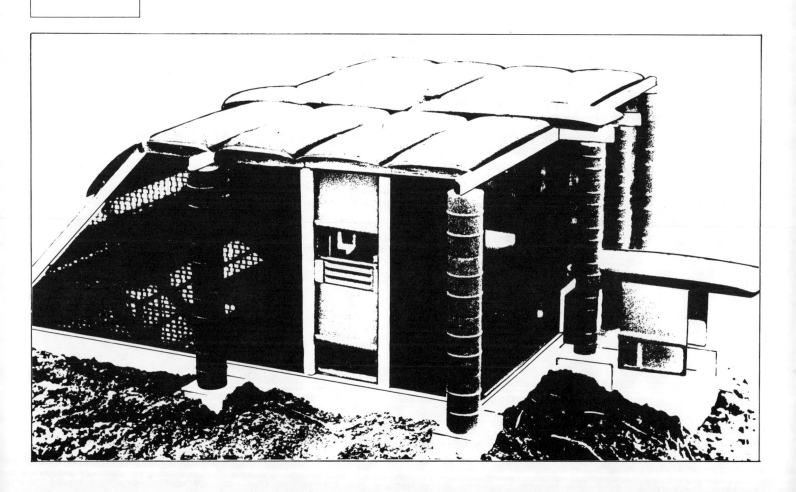

❝ Normally when a machine enters the life of civilizations, it spawns other machines, along with novel enterprises and institutions. A machine has bizarre powers to crossbreed, to become a host, a parasite, or a saprophyte living on dead matter. Radios and air-conditioning devices find new habitats within the automobile. Enormous compacting machines come into being to give a new form to deceased automobiles—and small compacting machines arrive to make neat packages of household trash. **❞**

Daniel J. Boorstin, *The Republic of Technology, 1978*

Product Eugenics: Design for Evolution

Alex Moulton put this point another way a couple of years later. He said, "There must be a compulsion within mankind to attempt the evolution of objects, as if life itself were being given to them."[1] The idea that the development and proliferation of products can be compared with that of natural species and organisms was mentioned in Chapter 3. In both cases the force of environment is what determines patterns of development and rates of change—in simple terms, the success or failure of the object, natural or otherwise. This concept of evolution has, of course, received much attention in recent years in a historical sense but surprisingly little as a design theory, even though scholars of evolution endlessly debate the significance of minor changes in the skull form of animals or reptiles in pursuit of evidence of functional adaptation. Fitness for purpose is painstakingly arrived at in the natural world by way of relative advantage, and it is equally clearly reached in man-made products by something similar. Take the case of the progressive extinction of the big car at the hands of the small, the clearest possible example of a change in the environment bringing about a change in the overall frequency of genotypes, with "organisms of a different appearance and function" the result.[2]

If the Gucci Cadillac, like *Tyrannosaurus Rex,* falls victim to changes in the environment, then surely this environment also can be deliberately changed in order to bring about desirable product evolutions. This notion is simple as well as accurate: it underlies the widespread effort to save the returnable bottle (a species faced with extinction) and to exterminate the tin-free steel (TFS) can, a species poised to swamp the market. The problem of implementation is twofold: the product environment is too weak, and opinions differ about what is a desirable evolution. Let us consider the TFS can.

This product species is expensive to make, can hold only carbonated (pressurized) drinks, and can be used only once. Its recycling value, unlike that of the aluminum can with which it is often confused, is very low and its reuse potential (under present arrangements) is zero. The production success of the TFS can is based on the fact that it maximizes output in an industry where labor costs have increased faster than any other production cost, and transport and storage costs are so high that the light, paper-thin pressurized container represents minimum material used for maximum packaging work performed. It fits the present environmental economics of the beer and beverage business perfectly, and, consequently, its frequency (in the genetic sense) is increasing in relation to all competitors. As aluminum scrap values rise, the tendency will be for aluminum to leave the container inventory altogether; if this happens, the TFS can will occupy the "evolutionary niche" vacated. The enforcement of bottle laws requiring the stockpiling of one-way containers will also favor the TFS can because it can be more easily crushed and stored in a smaller space than can its bimetal or glass competitors.

Thus, the present product environment, which called the TFS can into existence, now reinforces its status because it is the easiest way for the industry to come to terms with the cost pressures generated by commodity prices and environmental action. The canning industry is not offered an energetically or commercially sound way out of the nonreturn container impasse — nor, it must be noted, does it find one itself; instead it adopts the line of least resistance and minimum loss: the TFS can. This is a form of natural selection. If the TFS is not what we want from the canning companies, we must

change the environment creatively: there can be few clearer examples of the consequences of applying pressure to pointless ends.

The "natural selection" of the TFS can is neither the only nor the most serious of the evolutionary errors permitted by the invisible hand of the marketplace and the intermittently effective environmental lobby, but it is instructive that no primary or secondary use design solution has emerged. It may be that in a highly competitive market that is heavily dependent on mechanical handling equipment, no basic redesign of the TFS can is practical for some time to come; but this should not inhibit the development of second uses — as voids in construction concrete work, for example. It is paradoxical that bio-

88. Interior of the Americology plant in Milwaukee. This automated municipal solid waste processing facility came into operation in May 1977 with the intention of extracting marketable quantities of ferrous and nonferrous metals, glass, and fuel additive from the solid waste stream. Two years later 35 percent of the waste processed was still being trucked to landfill, although the fuel fraction, with 30 percent of the calorific value of coal, was being used in a special $4 million furnace built at the nearby Wisconsin Electric Power Company. The company-estimated cost for a similar facility in 1979 was $30-$40 million. In 1979 the Milwaukee plant was losing $3 million a year but expected to break even in 1981.

technology, the commercial application of the transfer of hereditary genes, should already be emerging as a multimillion dollar business with prospects for the bacterial leaching of coal from narrow seams, consumption of oil spills at sea, and conversion of grain into sugar whereas the design of multiple use product organisms — a much more primitive aspect of evolution — should be virtually ignored.

Designers could help to bring about "biological" transformations: they could teach a fifteen-year-old car to turn itself back into raw materials, make a nonreturnable bottle become part of a multistory building, or design several billion otherwise useless postconsumer TFS cans into a number of important jobs in construction or civil engineering. Fates and futures can be designed into products at much less expense than is required to dispose of them by other means. It takes a special kind of design process to do it, one protected from fashion and sell functions but exposed to overall energy budgets and full life-cycle costings. This type of design would, in overall energetic terms, approximate to biotechnology. Just as bacteria may in time produce a passable imitation of

Saran wrap without the consumption of so much as a watt of electricity, so could skillful secondary use design solve a resource depletion or disposal problem at only the manpower cost of the designer. "A little metal and a lot of thought" is a good engineering maxim; even more thought extending through successive uses, from raw material to final disposal, would be even better.

Today most of the design work in resource recovery is going into the development of doomsday machines capable of crushing, burning, and burying everything that we make. Even if energy is extracted from the process and a proportion of the raw material that went in is retrieved, the energy expended in forming the product, giving it a unique geometry and strength, is lost forever. Nor should the enormous energy demands of these processing facilities be ignored. A much more energy-efficient response to the rising tide of waste would be a whole design ethos based on prolonging product life, developing alternative and successive uses, and exploring material substitutions that would enable products to tidy up after themselves.

151

"A Brick That Holds Beer"

For reasons rooted in the disorganization of the product environment, there are few examples of such design ingenuity, but this does not mean that they do not exist or that "smart" products are not possible. Twenty years ago Alfred Heineken conceived a modest project to develop a smart beer bottle, by which he meant a bottle designed to do something after its contents had been drunk. In this case the bottle was to have become a brick in the wall of a house, and instructions for the metamorphosis were to have been on the label. The Heineken WOBO (short for "WOrld BOttle") had its genesis in a visit Heineken paid to the Caribbean island of Curacao in 1960. He went there as part of a world tour of Heineken facilities, but one of the things he saw was the immense quantity of beer bottles brought to the island with no economic means of return to the bottling plants from which they had come. The other thing he saw was a major housing shortage. Whether he actually saw houses made from bottles we do not know; what we do know is that on his return to the Netherlands he looked around for an architect to design what he called "a brick that holds beer."

Over the next three years the project went through various phases. At first, interlocking and self-aligning bottles were designed, in the (correct) belief that the need for mortar would rob the bottle wall of much of its cheapness and simplicity. Some effective building bottles

were too heavy and slow-forming to be economical in production, for modern bottling machines, like canning machines, produce bottles at the rate of thousands a minute, and fractions of a second in forming time can greatly affect production costs. Other bottles were rejected by Heineken's marketing people because they were too "ugly" or too "feminine" in appearance. In the end, the bottle selected for production was a compromise with everything except marketing requirements. Its appearance was squat and "masculine," but it could not be used vertically for building purposes (by far the strongest orientation for a bottle), and it required cement mortar bonding with a silicon additive in order to make a wall. In 1963 the order was given to produce 100,000 WOBO's in two sizes, 350 and 530 milliliters. (The size difference was necessary in order to bond the bottles when building a wall, in the same way as a half brick is necessary when building with bricks.)

The actual building carried out with WOBO's was anticlimactic: a small shed grandly called a summer house was erected first, with a corrugated iron roof and timber corner supports where the builder could not work out how to resolve the junction between necks and bases running in the same direction. A conventional glass window was placed in one wall. Some time later a timber double garage received WOBO siding. Both these structures were built on the Heineken estate at Noord-

90.

wijk, near Amsterdam. John Habraken, the architect who designed the WOBO, had originally intended to produce a dry-jointing, self-aligning bottle construction system with the roof framework assembled from Heineken shipping crates; in the end, all that was left of this idea was the name. Apart from a brief involvement with the ATIM/ATIP project a decade later (see p.143), Alfred Heineken apparently did no further development work on the concept of the world's first beverage container designed for secondary use.[3]

To those unfamiliar with the output figures and unit strengths routinely achieved in the bottling industry, this project might seem bizarre, but as Gernot Minke's experi-

ment (described in Chapter 7) showed, it was soundly based in principle. Not only is there a long history of building with bottles of one kind or another, but the Heineken patent searches revealed the existence of several multi-use bottles, including a French one dating from before World War II. It is a fact that bottle production greatly exceeds brick and concrete block output in all developed countries; even in many developing countries it represents an area in which production could be greatly increased without difficulty, provided some valuable second function, such as building, justified the expenditure involved. Furthermore, the strength requirements for pasteurizing and capping greatly exceed those for most simple types of construction.

91.

90 and 91. The final version of the WOBO. In this version the bottle is interlocking but requires mortar and is laid on its side, where it is weakest (**90**). The "Summer House" (**91**) was a test structure built from some of the 100,000 bottles produced in 1963. Later proposed uses for the remainder of the WOBO's included the SARBURO (**Fig. 82**) and the ATIM project (**Figs. 83** and **84**).

153

Despite its disappointing final design, the WOBO project had other economic advantages. Since its original distribution cost would be covered by the purchase price of the beer, the bottle as a construction element would have been parasitical upon an existing transportation and marketing system, thereby setting its real acquisition cost at zero, provided it was employed in the area in which it was marketed. Equally important was the potential embodied energy saving, which, at about 7,80 Btu per bottle, is written off every time a bottle is dumped or smashed. In this sense, for all its shortcomings, the WOBO was a sophisticated and intelligent design solution to what has emerged as a major environmental issue in the years since the project was abandoned. By providing a secondary use for so simple and prolific a product as a beer bottle, Heineken had at a stroke given it a value which — in the context of the developing markets for which it was intended — would have solved from the outset all disposal problems. In one simple product the WOBO showed a way to achieve metamorphosis and parasitism through design: a quantum leap in product evolution.

The Long-Life Car

About fifteen years after the inception of the Heineken project, another household name among manufacturers embarked upon a revolutionary departure from the conventional. The Porsche design office in Stuttgart, West Germany, world famous for the design of high performance sports cars, decided to reexamine the future prospect for automobiles in the light of the gloomy predictions of environmentalists and those concerned with the exhaustion of resources. Research indicated that automobiles were prime consumers of resources other than petroleum and that their short life (an average of ten years) and marginal recyclability threatened their continued availability in the years ahead. The problem of recyclability was growing in urgency, for studies carried out at Cornell University had already shown that the design of motor vehicles greatly hampered their dismantling and reprocessing by the scrap industry — so much so that often all the steel they contained was chemically sacrificed in order to retrieve the more valuable copper present in their wiring.[4] With the world scrap heap of automobiles exceeding 15 million units per year in the mid 1970s, the loss of high-grade steel, nonferrous alloys, rubber, plastic, and even engine oil was a significant and threatening increase in the already high environmental cost of private transport.

The Porsche response to this problem was ingenious. As part of a reduction in the amount of steel in their proposed car from 80 to 45 percent of its gross weight, the amount of recyclable alloy was increased from 5 percent to 40 percent. Together these changes reduced the percentage of irretrievable material in the vehicle from 70 to 35 percent. This significant improvement in resource recovery potential (or reproductive capability) was itself doubled by an extension of the planned life of the vehicle from ten to twenty years. Not only was the efficiency of scrap processing increased, but the volume of vehicles scrapped would be halved by doubling their life.

Inevitably the cost of the twenty-year, 180,000-mile car was greater than that of a conventional short-life vehicle, but only (according to 1976 projections) by about 30 percent. In any case, proposals were made for financing the car over nine years, which at then current interest rates would have brought its effective annual price down to about 15 percent below that of a conventional vehicle. In addition to its resource recovery and amortized cost advantages, the "long-life car," as the project was called, possessed provable energy advantages over conventional vehicles. Assuming a total mileage of 200,000 completed over twenty years, the proposed vehicle used only 35 percent of the embodied energy required by the three conventional cars necessary (on average) to reach this figure. Its fuel consumption offered no major advantage except in an aluminum-bodied model that achieved

92. Material Breakdown for a Conventional Car and Two LLC (Long-Life Car) Configurations

92, 93, 94, and 95. Porsche design office parameters for the material and energy performance of the long-life car project carried out by the company in 1975.

Conventional vehicle

2,200 lbs

16%
7%
3%
14%
60%

LLC utilizing mainly ferrous materials

2,261 lbs

15%
7%
2%
19%
57%

LLC utilizing mainly aluminum materials

1,813 lbs

17%
9%
33%
36%
5%

Steel

Cast iron

Aluminum

Plastics

Other materials

93. Function/Cost Analysis

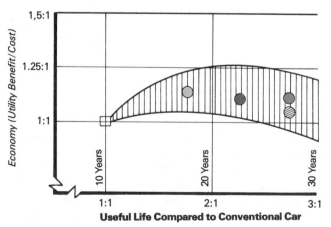

94. Overall Energy Consumption

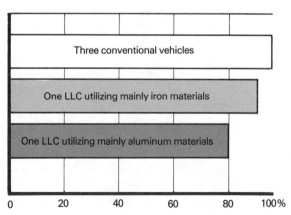

95. Overall Material Consumption

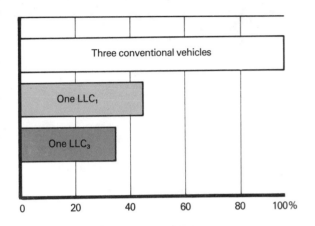

- ☐ CV; Conventional vehicle
- ◉ LLC$_1$: Vehicle with hot-dipped galvanized steel bodywork
- ○ LLC$_2$: As LLC$_1$ with increased part replacement
- ● LLC$_3$: Vehicle with aluminum bodywork
- ◍ LLC$_4$: Vehicle with stainless steel bodywork

higher figures by weight reduction.

The failure of this project even to advance to prototype stage (several alternative design studies were carried out) owed much to the kind of influence that stalled the earlier WOBO, although in this case there were strong objective reasons for the originators, the Porsche design office, not to take it any further themselves. In addition to the alleged damage that such a utilitarian departure might have done to the reputation of Porsche cars among those who buy them, there is also the undeniable fact that the environmental and systemwide benefits promised by the car required production on a large scale in order to have the desired effect: a scale far larger than any specialist manufacturer could attain. Until quite recently efforts were being made to establish the long-life car concept in a developing country where a native automobile industry could be grounded in this principle.[5]

The Newsprint Insulation Network

If the WOBO project demonstrated the possibility of parasitism and metamorphosis among consumer products, and the long-life car study suggested a means of achieving some kind of reproductive capacity comparable with that which exists in nature, the third example to be cited illustrates something akin to a food chain. Newspapers are of course a mass waste product, like cans, bottles, and automobiles. Indeed, their origins go back to the same explosion of productive power at the turn of the nineteenth century. In 1870 the paper-making industry could barely keep pace with rotary presses capable of turning out 18,000 newspapers an hour; by 1900 seven editions a day were common in metropolitan areas; and in 1927 the news of Lindbergh's flight across the Atlantic was able to call forth 25,000 tons of extra newsprint to meet public demand. Today nearly 40 percent by weight of household refuse consists of paper, half of it newsprint discarded after a life of one day.

The development of secondary uses for newspaper lagged far behind the booming market for newspapers themselves. Recycling of old newsprint began as a response to curtailed supplies during World War I in Europe and became a standard technique for the same reason during World War II. By the 1960s (according to some estimates) up to one-third of all paper was being de-inked and recycled, but still the waste value of the product remained low and subject to periodic glut and famine, with the result that no organized market comparable with that for scrap steel, aluminum, or copper existed. Environmentalists grew outraged at the scale of consumption of forest involved — 200 acres for the *New York Times* alone every Sunday, principally for short-life advertising. What was needed was either synthetic paper or some means of blunting the offensive contrast between trees cut down and waste paper blowing in the streets.

Newsprint as insulation has a surprisingly long history, but prior to the development of shredding and fluffing equipment for paper its secondary use was limited to the poor, who lined their clothes with it. Then in the 1970s with the rising cost of domestic heating fuel, this position changed and hundreds of small companies sprang into existence converting waste newsprint collected within the local community into bags of loose-fill insulation. Initially, the equipment required was not expensive; the paper was hand-sorted on arrival and fed into one or more grinding mills at a rate of about 150 pounds per minute per mill. From the mill the ground paper fragments were transported to a cyclone that extracted dust, and the fluffed, ground paper was then treated with boric acid and other fire-retardant chemicals and loaded into 30-pound bags for sale. This process — whereby the trees initially cut down to make paper for local news and advertising eventually found their way into attics and walls as permanent insulation instead of being burned or dumped — has, as even this abbreviated description makes clear, a compelling logic in resource conservation terms. The almost total loss represented by newsprint that is not recycled into new paper — and much newsprint is not, owing to difficulties in de-inking and problems with color printed papers — could thus be retrieved as a capital good economically — and locally to even the smallest communities.

Unfortunately for the logic of product evolution, the insulation market in the United States was dominated by two large corporations specializing in fiberglass, a substance in direct competition with the small companies' newsprint-based cellulose. Because the large corporations were centralized, established, and possessed of considerable lobbying power, they were able to express this competition in a most effective way. As the insulation market expanded in the late 1970s, the small, under-capitalized cellulose companies were forced to submit their product to increasingly stringent laboratory tests. Allegedly, the purpose was to eliminate fire risk, but it had the additional effect of driving many of them out of business because the cost and duration of the test procedures required to meet proliferating federal, state, local, and other regulations could only be met by increasing the cost of cellulose insulation until it became noncompetitive.

Because the cellulose insulation industry is by definition a local employer and a local distributor (the

96. Interior of a small cellulose insulation plant in Tallahassee, Florida, in 1979: a typical small facility based on local supplies of newsprint. The dust-extracting cyclone is in the foreground.

petroleum-based fiberglass industry is centralized and distributes over a wide area), the effects of its failure were localized too. In Florida by the spring of 1979 half the eighteen cellulose plants that had come into existence during the preceding five years had ceased production and were up for sale. As a result, the collection networks built up around them, often involving voluntary organizations and charity drives accumulating newspaper on an assumed market valuation, also collapsed, with much ill feeling. As the small proprietors who had invested up to a quarter of a million dollars in their plants looked around for buyers, the fiberglass corporations breathed a sigh of relief. Competition based upon the logical use of resources in a consumer society, whereby a high-volume, short-life product was fed into a second, much longer-life cycle as a form of storage in use, had proved no match for centralized economic muscle.

Toward A Ruthless Product Environment

Although one of the most obvious lessons to be learned from these three examples is that all either failed or appear to be failing in the process of disseminating their product, the facts surrounding their existence confirm another more important message. Both the WOBO and the long-life car were projects embarked on by corporations with a worldwide reputation and a well-established product; nor is the cellulose insulation industry a frivolous enterprise dependent on fashion or whim. In fact, all three examples are taken from the real world of business and production, where short-lived voluntary enterprise and wildly optimistic new departures are heavily discounted. How is it that such unorthodox projects found their way into this area? As we shall see, the real answer to this question is another: How did these projects find their way out of the "genetic pool"?

In every industry—as in every species in the natural world—there exists an almost infinite number of "genetic variations" available for production. These variants are the result of the application of thought to the processes of production, distribution, and consumption and take the form generally of *designs,* expressed as ideas, theories, patents, projects, prototypes, unused or abandoned production models, or even manufactured items stockpiled against future use. The WOBO, the long-life car, and cellulose insulation are examples of different states of evolution within this "genetic pool" in three different industries, with the last the most developed (being in actual use) and the second the least developed (being no more than a project). Projects or fledgling products are not confined to the beer and beverage industry, the auto industry, or the building industry; they exist in every field of production from machine tools to paper sleeping bags. In the canning industry, for example, there are (or have been) cans shaped like bottles, three-piece steel cans, three-piece bimetal cans, two- or three-compartment cans, aluminum cans, church-key-opening cans, vacuum cans, self-heating cans, pressurized cans, plastic containers designed to fit can-handling equipment, synthetic wooden cans, cans hand-soldered from sheet steel, and cans punched out like machine gun bullets from solid blocks of metal. In addition, this array of variations covers a range of sizes extending from 6-ounce beer cans to 55-gallon oil drums. These ideas, patents, and products of the canning industry constitute but one tiny part of the genetic pool of possibilities existing within industry as a whole, ready and waiting for a change in the product environment to call them forth in immense volume. The potential of secondary use, like the potential of waste as a whole, depends on just such an environmental change.

Like organisms, products evolve and adapt according to the rigors of the environment into which they are born:

they succeed or fail in competition, which is not merely a spur to efficiency but to evolution as well. Without it, no design evolution occurs, just as no species evolution takes place once a species has gained control of its environment. Indeed, it may be that the only substantive difference between product and natural evolutionary systems is one of efficiency: the product environment being weak and disorganized and readily overwhelmed by the frequency of products that do not integrate into the total energy economics of the system so that waste, pollution, and resource exhaustion ensue; whereas the natural environment retains its pitiless rigor, which no species can escape.

In an ideal world the invisible hand of the marketplace or the regulatory agencies, which are increasingly superseding the pricing mechanism as the arena for the "natural selection" of competing examples, should be able to filter out wasteful and inefficient examples like the TFS can, replacing it instead with the WOBO or constructing some chain of uses into which it would fit to economic advantage. In practice, neither does the job, partly through the inertia and lobbying power of the industries concerned and partly through the absence of coherent direction in what is still managed as though it were a gross growth economy, even though only net growth is still possible. In evolutionary terms this is perhaps the most crucial failure of our time, and it is wrong to lay the blame for it on the industries concerned. This situation has arisen not because "Detroit has cars that will do 100 miles a gallon, but they won't produce them," but because only the environment (however constituted) can *command* the production of such variations as a condition of the survival of the industry. Detroit *does* have cars that will do 100 miles a gallon, but the regulatory agencies do not know how to manipulate the product environment to bring them onto the market.

In great measure this failure is the result of ignorance of the existence of the industrial genetic pool on the part of those charged with the direction of regulatory and pricing policy. The sum of ideas, patents, projects, and prototypes within the genetic pool adds up to a complete taxonomy of metamorphic and adaptive possibilities that

97. The female of the ichneumon fly ("Rhyssa") boring with her oviposter through a fallen log to lay eggs in the larva of the giant saw-fly ("Sirex"), which has its burrow deep within the wood. When the eggs hatch, the larvae feed upon the tissues of the saw-fly larva.

162

should be at the service of policy makers, but in their ignorance of it they fear to lay too heavy a burden upon industry. In the placid atmosphere that ensues, the old product species degenerate, lose their powers of adaptation and metamorphosis, and lie ready victims to environmental change.[6]

The missing link between the extravagant waste production of consumer societies and the cycles of production, reproduction, and decay that preserve resources in the natural world lies in the file cabinets and microfilms of the patent offices and research laboratories of the world's corporations and universities. The genetic pool offers answers to the absence of product reproductive systems, to the absence of a man-made equivalent to the

carbon cycle, and to the absence of the wealth of complex interfaces between species and organisms that raises the systemic efficiency of the natural world far above anything yet achieved by our technology.

If biotechnology represents the impact of biology upon the processes of industrial production, then the rich contents of the industrial genetic pool represent its potential impact upon product design and resource recovery. Whereas in nature one species is used as a carrier for the growth and development of another, so by design could man-made products metamorphose from container to building component, from building component to raw material, from raw material back to container, or on to something else: any combination, any chain, any use but waste.

As children, we learn with fascination and horror how the female of the ichneumon fly bores through rotten wood to lay its eggs in the larva of the giant saw-fly, which has its burrow there. The eggs grow within the larva and, when they hatch, sustain themselves by eating it alive, taking care to consume only inessential tissue until the last. How much more sophisticated, ruthless, and economical is this interrelationship of species than any technological equivalent, except perhaps in the secret genetic pool of weapons of war. And yet such processes could be emulated with economic and resource recovery advantage if the leading roles were played by products instead of organisms. Supposing, for example, hazardous waste "Rhyssa" is piped to large parking garages where it is liberated to attack genetically coded vehicles of a predetermined age "Sirex." Once "Rhyssa" has been absorbed into the body of "Sirex," it begins to decompose all the nonrecyclable parts of the vehicle such as plastics, fabrics, and adhesives. Carefully, it leaves functional parts alone even though it migrates around the interior of the vehicle as a result of the vibrations induced by use. At a predetermined point "Sirex" gives a signal and must be driven directly to a material recycling center, where it abruptly disassembles into reusable parts and raw materials. At this exact point "Rhyssa" harmlessly vaporizes, having been neutralized by chemicals contained in the vehicle components it has consumed. Are such things possible? For science and technology they are things of the future to be sure, but the real proof that they can be done is the fact that relationships of this sort occur routinely in nature where they are forced into existence by an environment that permits only the most integrated systems to survive.

An inner consistency links such ideas as the WOBO, the long-life car, cellulose insulation, and the thousands of equivalent notions that lurk, conceived but not born, in the genetic pool of scientific and technological ideas. Because of the disparate industries from which these foetal notions emerge, there is as yet no linking field, no profession to assume responsibility.

What is required is a form of *product eugenics*, the breeding in captivity of successive generations of smart products to supersede their dumb predecessors. It is the role of the environment to enforce this desired evolution, and there is only one way that the product environment can be rendered coherent enough and rigorous enough for the purpose: a dramatic increase in the analytical and planning powers of the regulatory agencies coupled with the kind of draconian enforcement not seen since World War II.

What would happen if the regulatory agencies were conceded, by government fiat, their true analogical role as the arbiter of all products and wastes? If they issued drastic evolutionary specifications and imposed severe deadlines for compliance so that all emissions from manufacturers, whether in the form of products, waste products, or pollution, were obliged to take the form of chains or cycles without loose ends or resource losses. We know that this is possible in theory; we have grounds for suspecting that it is possible in fact. Why should we not demand it?

Conventional wisdom suggests that even the mildest pressures from the federal government generate higher consumer costs and lower production and shift yet more people into regulatory rather than productive jobs, thereby further decreasing the efficiency of the economic system. But this conventional wisdom is flawed for two reasons: it is heavily influenced by management rationalizations for inertia ("If it ain't broke, don't fix it"), and it is part of the penalty paid for a purely negative direction of regulatory policy — against waste, against pollution, against accidents, but not *for* a new system of energy accounting with far-reaching implications for the whole process of consumption.

If existing regulatory agencies were reconstituted or superseded by a new superagency, a Department of Product Evolution perhaps, armed with computer-modeled data on the totality of resources, production and reproduction capabilities, life-cycle costings, and waste disposal operations within the U.S. economy, then the results might be different. Such an organization would have at its fingertips an immense designing and planning capability, covering all patents held and all projects undertaken or contemplated in every industry. Its mode of technology assessment would be governed by true energy calculations, incorporating embodied, direct, operating, and disposal elements freely traded off one against the other in the pursuit of an optimum budget—and thereby fostering the most wonderful variety of ways and means to eliminate waste.

With the experience of recent years it is difficult to conceive of regulatory agencies as a source of economy and efficiency, but this problem does not so much proceed from the nature of regulation as from its unsystematic and incompetent use. For regulation to be successful, its goals must be clear and its rule unquestioned; where there is endless confusion about what constitutes real economy or real saving, where rules are compromised, subverted, or delayed, the analogy with the regulatory powers of the natural environment becomes a mockery. Much-criticized examples such as OSHA restrictions in building, 5-mile per hour bumpers, and bottle laws coincide historically with the existence of large corporations whose powers of evasion are multiplied by their multinationality, whose lack of real competition has stabilized markets to such an extent that their products lack adaptive power and must be protected by tariff barriers. None of this is the fault of regulation as a principle: during World War II the planning of production and the strict regulation of the consumer market brought forth a massive growth in industrial power. It is the fault of weak, fragmented, or nonexistent strategy, ignorance of the value or meaning of natural examples, and the imposition of unsound resource and energy controls. The kind of regulation the American industrialist and consumer has become used to neither cuts deep enough to improve systemic efficiency nor cuts shallow enough to avoid additional costs and additional layers of bureaucracy. Today public interest groups, government, and productive industry are locked in battle over details, many of them important to the environment to be sure, but none of them worked into a general strategy of resource utilization. Consequently, direction of the major flows of energy and materials through the economy is,

by inertia and default left to the tangential effects of conflict.

It is futile for industry to argue against regulation in principle because no other principle than regulation operates in nature: there is no alternative because no alternative exists. It is wrong for industries to seek, as they put it, to regulate themselves because a product environment controlled by products is as doomed as a natural environment controlled by species. It is equally futile for public interest groups to seek the suppression of industry and production because, like children's games, they "make a mess." The mess is part of the game and the game is part of childhood; being able to clean it up afterward is what makes it a game and not a harbinger of terminal disorder. Industrial production is as much a part of modern life as play is a part of childhood; both need to be circumscribed, neither can be suppressed without the creation of far worse evils.

It is no exaggeration to state that regulation of product species has become the central issue for a society that only ten years ago thrilled to plausible predictions of its own extinction by the end of the century. Regulation is essential and only one regulatory model, nature itself, has the clarity and sophistication to serve our complex, multivalent purposes. In nature species are so responsive to the rigors of the environment that regulation is almost subliminal. There is no conflict between the two in the sense that we understand the term because any such battle would be futile and short. Do species or individual creatures ever stand up against their environmentally determined fate? We do not know, and in any case it does not matter because the issue is never in doubt. Only ingenuity in the navigation of an unforgiving environment pays dividends in nature, and the reward for ingenuity is the ultimate species good of survival. With us matters are differently arranged: with weak regulatory agencies, pressure groups, and corporations operating according to a system of shifting alliances and retrospective judgments, the result is a kind of economic wildlife park with no rangers—a battleground in which corporations fight a perpetual rearguard action in defense of fat, wasteful, obsolete products and short-run waste disposal expedients. Pressure groups ride un-predictable outbursts of public indignation, which sooner or later run out of steam. And regulatory agencies walk a fine line between whistle blowing and playing politics.

There can be no doubt that this pattern is doomed. It cannot lead to the human species triumphing over the natural environment, for that is impossible. The only feasible result is that the grisly tide of undigested waste and pollution will finally suppress us and all our works. The time has come to restore the primacy of the environment, not by reverting to agrarian simplicity but by constructing a product environment of sufficient rigor to compel the evolution of sustainable patterns of consumption. Design has a role of incalculable importance to play here, for it is the means whereby even the most irresponsible fripperies of Western life can be made to come to terms with evolution and the need to pay their way.

Notes

1. Alex Moulton, "Improving Existence," *The Times* (London), 18 February 1981. Moulton is an English designer of suspension systems for cars, the inventor of a new type of bicycle, and the patentee of a bicycle that can be folded into a suitcase.
2. The quote is from James M. Ford and James E. Monroe, *Living Systems: Principles and Relationships* (New York: Canfield Press, 1974). In full it reads: "If the environment should change, the overall frequency of genotypes would change and organisms of a different appearance and function result. It is quite correct then to treat evolution as a change in gene frequencies." It is quite correct also to treat the rise of small cars as a product-evolutionary change.
3. In a conversation with Alfred Heineken in January 1973 he expressed his conviction that the WOBO would still one day make the cover of *Time* magazine. It is a pity that his faith in it was not sufficient to override marketing fears and to test-launch it in a small export market — in Chile, for example, where the opportunity arose during the Allende administration. The only full account of the WOBO project is to be found in Martin Pawley, *Garbage Housing* (New York: Halsted, 1976).
4. *The Recycle of Auto Hulks Vols. I and II,* Program on Science, Technology and Society (Ithaca: Cornell University Press, 1970). This pioneering study made several intelligent proposals for the modification of vehicle design and assembly in order to permit easier stripping and resource recovery, most of which have been ignored by the industry. They included fastening techniques based on different magnetic suscepti-bilities so that cars could be disassembled with pulsed magnetic fields, shear fasteners designed to break if the hulk was dropped vertically from 20 feet, easily detachable surface wiring looms, modular assembly of all recyclable components, and so on. The only widely accepted recommendation has been the substitution of louvered steel or plastic panels for chrome radiator grilles.
5. This account of the Porsche *Langzeitauto* project is taken from Dr. Ing. Ferry Porsche, *We at Porsche* (New York: Doubleday, 1976); from Ernst Fuhrmann, "The Long-Life Car," *Futures,* June 1979; and from correspondence with Dr. Hermann Braess of the Porsche design office. The full report on all phases of the project is published in German under the title *Forschungsprojekt Langzeitauto* (Bonn: Bundesministerium fur Forschung und Technologie, December 1976).
6. It is evidence of the extent of mishandling in the product environment that many manufacturers seek to diversify away from regulated areas rather than comply with repressive and contradictory controls. With multinational corporations this tendency is expressed in the transfer of production facilities overseas or the sale of an obsolete production plant rather than replacing it with a new one. This is not an argument for less regulation but rather for more, but with a more rewarding goal than the ultimate suppression of the product.

9 Building for Tomorrow

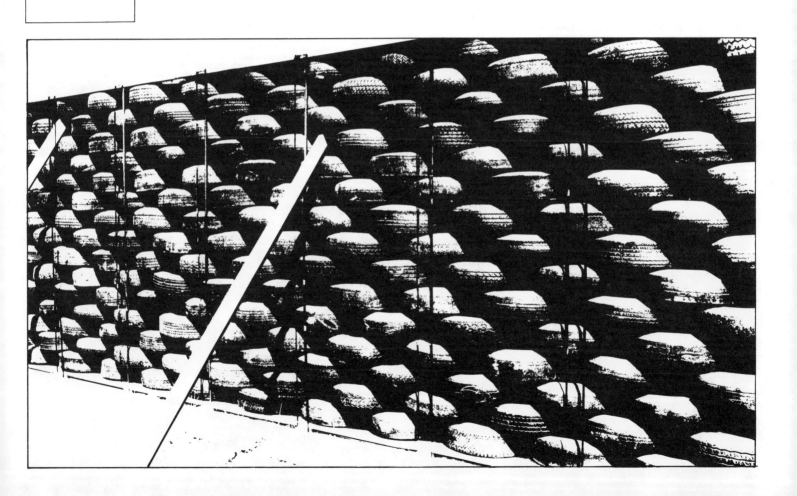

❝ It was my growing conviction that there could be no architecture of our time without the prior acceptance of scientific and technical developments. I have never lost this conviction. Today, as for a long time past, I believe that architecture has little or nothing to do with the invention of interesting forms or with personal inclinations. True architecture is always objective and is the expression of the inner structure of our time, from which it stems. **❞**

Mies van der Rohe (quoted in *Mies van der Rohe at Work,* by Peter Carter, 1964)

Building for Tomorrow

It is axiomatic that anything can be used to build with, provided it is available in sufficient quantity. This is not a newly minted aphorism but, as a moment's thought will show, a very ancient one. In the very long history of building the most unpromising materials — rocks, trees, sheepskin, snow, mud, and straw — have been pondered over, experimented with, abandoned, taken up again, and finally developed into building materials so common as to be unquestioningly accepted by generation after generation. All traditional building materials grew up this way, not because they were especially suitable but because they were plentiful in the areas where they were used.[1]

With the coming of the machine age, the production of ancient materials was first mechanized, then synthesized, and finally overtaken by floods of substitutes with no natural counterpart. When this happened, the requirement of plentifulness was itself transformed. In urban areas there might be little stone or slash pine, but there were building stores where sheets of plywood and attenuated strips of lumber were shipped by manufacturers. The age of specialized building materials destabilized the very basis of construction until wood, brick, and stone no longer looked traditional and the only things that did were made out of fiberglass. Esoteric materials such as aluminum became commonplace although they were used in thin, carefully designed sections intended to extract the maximum service from the smallest possible quantity. Glass grew from a small, thin, uneven, indistinct translucency to a story-high double- or treble-skinned crystal transparency that was window, wall, and architecture all in one. Steel too replaced cast iron as a complete constructional system, with cold- or hot-rolled standard sections bolted or welded together into immense skyscrapers or ground-hugging factories. In and around all this were the truly synthetic materials, poured from a laboratory test tube to be rolled, stamped, or cut into shape for a thousand interstices. Finally, there were whole buildings, sometimes cut into two or three pieces for ease of delivery but built whole in a factory and sold off a lot, like a car.

In this world of centralized specialization, building became an assembly industry based on lines of supply as narrow and vulnerable as those of an invading army. Cut off from their Red Ball Express of purpose-made, dimensionally integrated panel systems, modern builders could do nothing. Sometimes they got stuck like this in the Third World; then they had to make the roads and factories first and put up their buildings much later.

Yet because of the wonderful skill and ingenuity of the whole system, building still got cheaper. For a few years after World War II about a third of the houses built in America were put up by their owners, using specialized building materials like precut lumber, plywood, and asphalt shingles, but with the owners doing the labor themselves. Twenty years later almost nobody did this: and if they did not do it with housing, we can be sure that all the other more expensive or gigantic building types were not self-built either. By the early 1970s the specialist building industry in the U.S. had cut the proportion of the total price of a new house attributable to all materials by 10 percent over 1950 — and the houses were bigger and better too.

But in the process attenuation and *ersatz* had between them skinned the old materials down to nothing. Ordinary stick-built houses where the strength was once calculated in the studs, now took the sheathing into account too — and as a result the studs shrank to matchsticks. In bigger buildings such as offices and hotels, so much fusion of materials took place that a composite floor slab incorporating heating, lighting and air conditioning above a false ceiling added up to half the material cost of the whole building. Reduced man hours, integrated component assemblies, dry-jointing techniques, and higher maintenance cost kept new construction in its place on the inflationary curve. Compared with 100 years before, building cost less, but it was less too: an uneasy industry neither big nor small, utterly dependent on interest rates and borrowed money, with a product that was not cheap and throwaway or expensive and durable but

something infinitely worse — obsolete.

To say this is not to say that high-performance buildings, cheap buildings, or beautiful buildings are no longer made. It is to say that modern buildings have assumed the character of impediments to economic life rather than instruments to facilitate its pursuit; and this applies from the simplest tract house to the largest shopping mall. Because they now act as envelopes for the process of consumption, all buildings have become larger than they used to be. Like cars they have developed into extraordinarily complex devices; but without the elasticity offered by the enormous production capacity of the automobile, they are slow to respond to changing circumstances. Worse still, the bureaucratic complications that surround their erection are rapidly being matched by difficulties in demolition and even change of use. Inflation and unsatisfied demand make buildings appreciate rather than depreciate, and to put up a sizable urban building requires a lead time on the order of five years or more. As a result, the mass of steel, glass, aluminum, copper, wood, and plastic that finds its way into such buildings becomes walled up, buried alive in a complex whose active life is determined by financial considerations utterly unrelated to the energetic cost of the building itself.

Housing: Equity or Energy?

The effects of this process on the simple utility of construction can be most clearly seen in the case of housing, where the figures are readily available. Assessed demographically, the need for new housing in the United States can be derived from household formation rates, population migrations, changes in employment opportunities, patterns of urbanization, and changes in the age structure of the population. Such data show that demand will rise steadily to the mid-1990s because while the proportion of the population age twenty-five to forty-four rose by only 2.3 percent between 1960 and 1970, it rose by 30 percent between 1970 and 1980 and will rise by 35 percent before 1990. Since this age group forms more than three-fourths of all new households, it represents the principal target for new housing. But in practice, even if demand was not actually higher than the age-group rate suggests (because of the steady growth in single-person households), the housing industry still cannot serve it. The reason is that market demand and demographically assessed need are quite different things.

As Table 21 shows, it is one thing to announce the need for a massive housing program on demographic grounds but another to make it connect with the financing arrangements of the construction industry in its present form. In Los Angeles, one of the most expensive housing areas in the country, the year 1980 saw builders and developers fighting a rear-guard action against

Table 21. Effect of Interest Rates on House Purchase Feasibility

Interest Rate Percentage	Percentage of U.S. Households Able to Buy
5	56
6	51
9	41
10	38
14	24
18	11
21	2

Note: This table is based on a constant ratio of earnings to house prices.

Source: U.S. Dept. of Commerce, NAHB Economics Dept., 1977 (percentages extrapolated by the author)

housing demand and rent control ordinances, even as their own product — priced in the mid-hundreds of thousands — aimed unerringly for resale or the foreign buyer with equity or cash to plow into his or her purchase. The following advertisement is typical of housing industry product at a time of acute housing need.

The homes of Foxboro Heights in Laguna Niguel have their architectural roots deep in the long ago. In the springtime of our American heritage. In the beautiful homes that dot the thick forests between the Rappahannock and the James, the crannied Hudson River Valley, the woodland clearings of Vermont and the breezeswept shores of Maine. They are

large homes. With architectural details that long ago faded from common usage. There are upstairs verandahs, entry doors with tympanum fanlights, clerestory dormers, chamfered cornerposts, window shelves and latticed Yorkshire lights.[2]

This is, of course, the language of investment rather than of performance, but the housing industry has been subsumed by the investment value of its scarce product to such an extent that it has come to live in a world of money, hyperbole, and gross product stagnation. Housing is no longer functional as a service because its function is to make money for its customers by maintaining demand not by satisfying it. Even the most efficient branch of the industry, the mobile home sector whose entire product is assembled in factories, has fallen prey to the same deformation so that what were once lean, spare, and minimal truckable buildings are now ornate builder's look-alikes standing on block foundations and mortgaged like ordinary houses. The whole industry is geared to serve the needs of home-owning households eager to trade up and spend their equity every year or so. But how well does it serve the needs of the 42 million Americans who will reach the age of thirty between 1980 and 1990? The number of house sales rose from 2.9 million in 1973 to 5.1 million in 1977, but the number of new houses coming onto the market declined and is now well below the old norm of 2 million a year. The boom in house sales was a boom in resales, a paper shuffle.

It is of course true that the housing industry is not the whole construction industry, and other sectors are less paralyzed by a mountain of debt on the one hand and a mountain of equity on the other. But housing accounts for more than 40 percent of all new building and nearly 40 of all energy consumed by building. Single family housing alone takes three times as much energy as office building (which is much more energy intensive), and all housing takes twice as much as industrial building, which is the second largest category. The poor performance of housing is crucial, even if it is bettered by the commercial and industrial sectors of the industry, because it brings the average down. The fact that a steel-building prefabricator can computer-design and produce a 43,000-square-foot clear-span industrial building with 80 tons of steel section and 50 tons of light cladding *in one day* does show how advanced parts of the industry have become,[3] but the industrial sector overall, including farm service buildings and warehouses, accounts for only a quarter of all new construction. For the bulk of the industry the problem is low productivity, cost, and delay—difficulties that have been turned into dubious virtues in housing but nowhere else.

The Worldwide Failure of Construction

Nor are the deficiencies of the construction industry confined to the domestic market. As every sixth-grader knows, the dimensions of the world need for building, particularly housing, reach far beyond the capabilities of all the housing industries in the world, not just in the United States. Urban populations alone will, by the year 2000, add up to over 3 billion people; and to house them adequately by that date will require the construction of ninety cities the size of Philadelphia every year. Nor can anything prevent these cities from coming into existence, whether they are planned or just grow out of those which already exist. In 1950 there were only seventy cities in the world with a population greater than one million; today there are more than 150. By the year 2000 there will be nearly 300 in the Third World alone. Unless something unprecedented occurs, these cities will have enormous squatter populations, half the total or more, and this "informal sector" will constitute a perpetual threat to the stability of every country in which such cities are found.

And yet what the billion homeless people of the *barriadas* and *campamentos* want is not impossible to supply or, at least, has not proved to be so in the developed economies of the West. The problem is that it does not even register on the scale of market demand. They want a civilized life with jobs and homes they are prepared to build themselves if necessary; the tragedy is

that the threshold of construction costs is far above their heads, so the industry can make no response to this enormous area of basic need. It is of course conventional to reverse this statement, claiming that the income of the *pobladores* is too low, but this is merely an evasion to disguise where the blame really lies. If, as the housing industry in the United States does, the government of a developing country defines housing demand as the sum of people earning enough to be lent the money to buy, then there is (against all the evidence) a lack of demand. If, on the other hand, it accepts the evidence of the number of homeless or ill-housed people within its borders, then there is a line of customers that literally encircles the globe, and there is something very wrong with the construction industry.

By accepting the parameters of conventional construction as the limits to all constructive power, and by accepting the cost of conventional construction as the only price at which building can take place, we have come to respect the limits of an obsolete industry as though they were laws of nature. The resource base of the industry today is inadequate for its global task. It must move to the mine of the new materials generated by industry and consumption.

How else are the homeless people of the Third World to be housed but by a revolutionized construction industry? It is not so much naïve as cynical to talk about a reversion to traditional methods when the crisis is already on a scale never seen before. In Cairo alone the density of population is 75,000 persons per square mile, and all open spaces in the city are carpeted with squatters, including the cemeteries. Even the relatively high productivity of the industrialized housing systems developed in Eastern Europe after World War II has proved unequal to the task. Where such housing has been built, it has been overwhelmed by population growth, poor maintenance, and poor administration; it has always been too little and too late. In Egypt the Soviet development plan, which relied on prefabricated housing, could not even start building until the hydroelectric potential of the Nile, in the form of the gigantic Aswan dam, was

available to power the production machinery. There, as in other countries, the delay proved fatal to the strategy.

Industrialized housing, by far the most productive sector of the industry, needs skilled labor, energy, and good transportation — all the industrial infrastructure of a modern state. Without it, errors and delays pile up, and discredit is the ultimate result. The Third World is the graveyard of prefabrication programs. Their successor has been the site and service project, often no more than a 5,000-square-foot lot with a pit latrine and permission to build your own home — which amounts to a frank admission of the incompetence of the construction industry in the face of overwhelming demand. So great has been the failure of specialist construction that this is now the

98 and 99. A *campamento* in Chile, typical and better than most (**98**) and the ruins of a concrete public housing project in Puerto Rico (**99**). The Third World is the graveyard of prefabrication programs, and its squatter settlements are an endless indictment of the conventional construction industry.

98.

de facto housing policy of the developing world.

Against all likelihood this deindustrialized building policy has not been a failure. Unerringly the *bricoleurs* of the squatter settlements have turned to the waste products of industry and consumption to make good the inadequacies of building programs. In all developing countries there exists a massive black market network covering not only hijacked construction materials such as cement or galvanized steel roofing but also packing crates, boxes, frames, bags, containers, and packaging of all descriptions. In the infinite graduations of permanence of the squatter settlement, where land is seized and tenure may be uncertain for years on end, there is a market for all possible building materials from sheets of plastic to punctured oil drums. What does get built is as much a function of the variety of consumer goods imported as of the small quantities of purpose-made building materials that find their way onto the black market. One survey, carried out by Ahmedabad Municipal Corporation in India in 1976 showed that out of 81,000 huts and shelters in a squatter settlement within city limits, no less than 63 percent were roofed with "tiles" made from steel cans of various kinds whereas only 12 percent were roofed with cheap building materials such as asbestos cement or corrugated iron.[4] Clearly, notwithstanding low per capita income and the small consumer market relative to population size, building materials adapted from packaging and containers origi-

99.

175

nating half the world away are available in larger quantities and at lower prices than specialist items, in India at least. Even without organization for the purpose, the production success of the consumer industries as purveyors of building materials is already a global phenomenon.

Of course, this is not to suggest that the critical housing problems of the developing countries have been solved by the abdication of the construction industry. The demographic basis of the problem in explosive urbanization promises that it will continue to worsen until measures appropriate to its scale are taken. What has happened is that events have forced an evolutionary move from specialized construction toward a larger resource base—the reservoir of waste and short-life products generated by the process of development itself—and it is this shift which should be regarded as a portent. It is an indication that perhaps the day of the construction industry as a specialist enterprise is over, and, like radio (also once an industry in itself), it will now become part of a larger production unit analogous to the world of electronics.

If construction in the Third World were to cease to be an industry that imported or manufactured components to build with and became instead an assembly skill taking resources from any number of available suppliers in agriculture, industry, or consumption, then it might begin to improve upon the ingenuity of the *bricoleur.* At

100. Cans on the move for secondary use in India.

present, construction and consumption compete for the same offshore currency: if consumption won, then perhaps construction could claw back material by way of secondary use.

The size of the consumer sector differs so widely in different developing countries that it is difficult to predict the effect of such a deliberate expansion. In Chile in 1972, when three-fourths of the population was urbanized and nearly 2 million were living in slums and squatter settlements, the *Unidad Popular* government considered a number of unorthodox housing strategies in order to boost the annual construction industry rate of about 60,000 homes a year. Eventually, it decided upon both a native timber panelized system and East European style prefabrication using imported equipment, neither of which made much contribution before the coup of September 1973, but the idea of a consumer-based emergency housing system was briefly evaluated, as described and illustrated in Chapter 7.

In Chile at the time, the entire consumer market operated at a very low per capita turnover. Production of containers and packaging was about 4 percent of the then current U.S. level, and automobile ownership was even lower. Nonetheless, the possibilities for increasing

production in both these areas were very high since native output of steel, glass, wood products, and plastics was actually being held back as a result of the loss of export markets, and vehicle production had temporarily ceased for lack of imported mechanical components. With the use of some of the techniques described in the last chapter, it would have been possible to justify a doubling of selected packaging output (paperboard, fiberboard, glass bottles, and cans) by feeding it into housing. Similarly, the production of small Citroen panel vans could have been restarted with the stimulus of using the body components as a housing system. Since any housing resulting from this program would have been additional to the 60,000 units contracted through the construction industry, the political benefits of even marginal success would have been considerable, but as the plan was not taken up, neither its pitfalls nor its rewards came to light. Short of unforeseen technical difficulties, labor shortages, or other problems, it seemed likely at the time that containers and packaging could provide about 6,000 units in the Santiago metropolitan region, and the Citroen project might have yielded up to 10,000 metal housing units a year—a joint increase of as much as 25 percent.

Matching Global Need with Global Supply

Source: Author's estimate

If the expansion of the consumer sector for construction purposes in a small developing country could produce a theoretical improvement in housing output of 25 percent, there are strong reasons for believing that in a country with a highly developed consumer culture such as the United States, similar adaptive processes could (if necessary) supplant the housing industry altogether. In embodied-energy terms this is certainly true, for the containers and packaging produced for the food and beverage market alone account for 600 trillion Btu a year (enough energy to build 800,000 houses). The addition of other short-life adaptable products such as refrigerators, washing machines, etc., as well as valuable wastes such as sulfur brings the total of house equivalents to over 2 million. For the purposes of this argument, however, it is unnecessary to promote such a substitution merely to show in outline that it could be done, for the first conclusion here is that any large-scale housing program conceived along lines appropriate to the global nature of the housing crisis must start from an evaluation of what *is* produced in volume—as opposed to what might be, or might have been, in an era of cheap energy and unlimited growth.

As even the limited selection in Table 22 shows, world production of short-life consumer products is already so greatly in excess of even the most prolific of conventional building materials that the trash of our gen-

Table 22. Estimated World Production of Some Volume Items

Commodities	Units per Year (billions)
Steel, bimetal, and alum. cans	320
Glass bottles, all types	160
Building bricks, all types	50
Concrete blocks	35
Vehicle tires	1
Private cars	0.025
Permanent houses	0.015

eration has no alternative but to become the acknowledged building resource of tomorrow, not only in the *barriadas* of the Third World but also in the United States. All that is necessary is the development of a new tradition of vernacular building based on the unique properties of these waste materials and a new building technology designed to ensure that their performance is adequate. These two processes have already begun in locations as far removed from one another as the site and service settlements of the developing countries and the resource recovery laboratories and universities of the West. As the cost of the old specialized materials and techniques rises beyond the reach not only of the Latin

American *pobladore* but of the middle-class American hoping to buy a home of his own, so will the wastes generated by the process of consumption find their way into the fabric of all our buildings. It is ironic but certainly not unjust that this process should have begun in the squatter settlements of Asia, Africa, and Latin America, only finally to find its place where the mass production of waste really began.

Given the present pattern of energy flows and resource movements in the U.S. economy, the building represents the least exploited, most undeveloped mechanism for the storage in use of large quantities of waste material that might otherwise be diffused irretrievably into the environment. Building from aluminum, steel, glass, or plastic waste would, in fact, constitute a form of investment far more valuable than any recycling program at present rates of retrieval. Thus, for example, if standard storage buildings were to be built from 100-pound bales of scrap aluminum, van or car bodies, glued bottles, cans, tires, or any other suitably energy-intensive waste, such waste buildings could be sized and graded according to their ultimate energy potential. It might then be possible to speak of a 6.5-billion Btu aluminum building (160 tons of aluminum) or a 15-billion Btu tire building (15,000 tires). Each of these structures, a temporary store of energy-intensive material as well as a multipurpose shelter, would play an economic role as a resource reserve to damp down price fluctuations. Tires could play this part well because of their high petroleum content, every year's discard representing 1.5 billion gallons of oil. Compared with the heavy rate of loss in recycling programs and bottle laws, this method would produce tangible benefits on a much larger scale. A 6.5-billion Btu aluminum building erected in 1973, when the recycling price for aluminum was only 10 cents a pound, would have represented $32,000 in scrap value. Six years later, when the recycling price had risen to 35 cents a pound, its value would have been a corresponding $112,000. Left to the vagaries of the recycling market, the hypothetical 6.4 million cans of 1973 would have suffered a progressive annual diminution to disappear altogether long before the end of the decade.

It is of course true that to some extent this type of calculation can be applied to the quantities of aluminum, steel, rubber, and plastic used in conventional building. But in normal building practice such materials are not often sufficiently concentrated or sufficiently easy to retrieve to make the process economical as a storage system. What is proposed here is the progressive substitution, initially in certain simple building types, of a new type of waste construction with energy conservation through storage in use as its primary aim. It should be possible to offset, for example, part of the 57 trillion Btu of energy consumed annually in the construction of warehousing by perhaps 5 trillion Btu worth of stored-in-use aluminum building, or, alternatively, part of the 460 trillion Btu consumed in the construction of industrial buildings by 90 trillion Btu worth of stored-in-use petroleum in the form of tires.

With the passage of time this technique might be expanded to include more complex building types, notably housing, with the ultimate aim of involving the whole built environment in the useful storage of refined resources. *By this means, instead of acting as an inert envelope for consumption distanced from the central logic of its operations, building could become an integral part of the industrial resource processing mechanism, with every structure playing a valuable part in resource conservation and economic life.*

Not the least of the virtues of such a system would be the manner in which it would reinforce and justify the process of consumption rather than loading it with further costs and restrictions, as is the case with almost all conservationist measures today. Notwithstanding the zeal of planners and regulators, it is not practical politics to promote any diminution in the supply of goods and services in the richest country on earth. Restraint under extreme circumstances or for the achievement of some visible goal is possible, but a general withdrawal from consumption will be fought every inch of the way. In view of the richness of the genetic pool of the consumer industries and the variety of strategies that can be applied from a position of wealth as opposed to one of poverty, such reluctance is justified. Academic and polit-

179

ical propagandists to the contrary, the supposed "futility" of the consumer lifestyle draws immigrants from the four corners of the earth.

How much wiser, then, instead of playing a cliff-hanging game with austerity and regulation, to attempt to loop the process of consumption back upon itself now while it is still charged with material wealth and economic energy. It is in this sense that the building as accumulator—the largest passive consumer of resources in our economic system—could break free from its traditional role as a capital good and become instead, not merely a depreciating production tool (as are the most efficient industrial buildings today) but part of a fluid, temporary assemblage of energy-intensive matter, ready at any time to disgorge resources needed for some other process or product. This quickening and intensifying of the economic life of buildings and the materials of which they are made—an endless process of construction and demolition absorbing and returning the full force of energy flows within the economy—would become the counterpart in a technological society of the effortless *insubstantiality* of preindustrial nomadic life.

The prime tool in any such effort to convert the ancient art of building into a modern science of resource conservation would have to be product eugenics, the breeding under regulatory agency control of the new generation of "smart" products, input-output chains, and ingenious secondary uses presently languishing in the

101 and 102. Two images of the potential of secondary use and storage in use. The industrial building by Milton Keynes Development Corporation, England (**101**), has siding based on van body techniques and manufactured in the auto industry—an industry presently hurt by recession but apparently unable to diversify into construction. The tire wall (**102**) represents a starting point for storage in use. Each tire represents a million Btu of embodied energy.

101.

180

genetic pool of unemployed ideas. Without such controlling strategies as design evolution could bring to bear, the difficulties of building would defeat waste substitution or at least rob it of its potentially enormous economic significance. With it, product eugenics could become the basis for an architecture of the future — a vital integrative art based on the totality of productive output in all its forms, from field wastes to industrial diamonds, and also an applied science based on the most advanced techniques of resource recovery and chemical transformation. Here would be a discipline with space for genius in unsuspected combinations and room for competence in the detailing of complex yet dismantlable assemblies whose components arrive from branches of industry and fields of production united only by their high output.

Under the rubric of this twenty-first century architecture, the act of building could leap from the Stone Age to what Mies van der Rohe called "the inner structure of our time," to seize an evolutionary role in the organization of the human society of the future. In time, the design and construction of buildings would become an economic reflex, like the stockpiling of grain, or coal, or valuable minerals today but with the additional social value of space enclosure. To turn our literally massive weight of buildings into accumulators of refined material energy would be truly building for tomorrow, for unlike our present architecture, it would be a sustainable system, a true instrument of human survival.

102.

Notes

1. This axiom is doubly important in dealing with waste or secondary use materials because their design continually evolves and changes. In 1963 the use of beer crates as the roofing system for the projected WOBO house was vetoed because it was believed that baling or gluing bottles together would soon become the normal means of packaging. Nearly twenty years later this development still has not come about but shrink wrapping, unknown at that time, is common. Conversely, the switch from synthetic rubber to plastic tires or from steel to plastic strapping, or the replacement of the glass bottle by the plastic bottle may come sooner than is expected. Either way the axiom still holds. If it is strong enough to be transported from one side of the country to the other, some kind of construction method can be devised for it. The strength requirements for building and packaging are surprisingly close.

2. *Los Angeles Times*, Real Estate Supplement, 13 April 1980.

3. This performance refers, of course, to the design and manufacture of the frame, purlins, roofing sheets, siding and ancillary envelope components, and their dispatch from the plant. Assembly requires a concrete slab, services, and other preliminaries that take more time, so the average time from order to completed building is about five weeks. This is still impressive in view of the enormous enclosed floor area — equivalent to thirty single family houses. These data are based on the typical performance of American Buildings Corp., Eufaula, Alabama, in 1979.

4. Details of this survey were contained in "The Unbalanced Equation," an unpublished paper delivered by Kirtee Shah of the Ahmedabad Action Study Group to the United Nations expert group meeting on the improvement of slums and squatter settlements held in Nassau, Bahamas, in February 1977.

Bibliography

The bibliography is in two sections, the first covering sources for Chapter Two, *Waste in America,* and the second covering general sources.

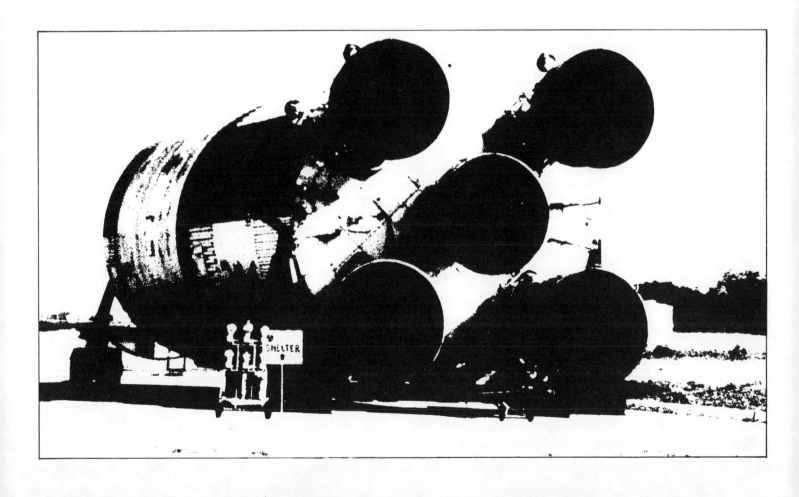

Bibliography/Chapter 2: Waste in America

Bond, Richard G., and Conrad P. Straub. *Handbook of Environmental Control Vol. II: Solid Waste.* Cleveland: CRC Press, 1973.

Brown, Michael. *Laying Waste: The Poisoning of America by Toxic Chemicals.* New York: Pantheon, 1980.

Clifton, James R., Paul W. Brown, and Geoffrey Frohn-dorff. *Survey of Uses of Waste Materials in Construction in the United States.* Washington, D.C.: National Bureau of Standards, 1977.

Darnay, Arsen, and William E. Franklin. *Salvage Markets for Materials in Solid Wastes.* Washington, D.C.: Environmental Protection Agency, 1972.

Down, C. G., and J. Stocks. *Environmental Impact of Mining.* New York: Halstead, 1977.

Loehr, Raymond C. *Pollution Control for Agriculture.* New York: Harcourt Brace Jovanovich, Academic Press, 1977.

Skitt, John. *Disposal of Refuse and other Waste.* New York: Halstead, 1972.

Small, William E. *Third Pollution: The National Problem of Solid Waste Disposal.* New York: Praeger, 1971.

Szekely, Julian, ed. *The Steel Industry and the Environment.* New York: Marcel Dekker Inc., 1973.

Van Tassel, Alfred J., ed. *Environmental Side Effects of Rising Industrial Output.* Lexington, Mass.: Heath, 1970.

Wilson, D. G., P. Foley, and R. Wiesman. "Demolition Debris: Qualities, Composition and Possibilities for Recycling." In *Proceedings of the Fifth Mineral Waste Utilization Symposium.* Chicago, 1976. Summarized in Clifton, Brown, Frohndorff, *Survey of Uses.*

Bibliography/General

Adler, Cy A. *Ecological Fantasies: Death from Falling Watermelons.* New York: Green Eagle Press, 1973.

Aplet, Jo Anne H. *The Uses of Completed Sanitary Landfills.* Unpublished paper. UCLA School of Architecture and Urban Planning, 1976.

Barringer, Edwin C. *The Story of Scrap.* Washington, D.C.: Institute of Scrap Iron and Steel Inc., 1947.

Boorstin, Daniel J. *The Republic of Technology: Reflections on our Future Community.* New York: Harper & Row, 1978.

Borkin, Joseph. *The Crime and Punishment of I. G. Farben: The Birth, Growth, and Corruption of a Giant Corporation.* London: André Deutsch, 1978.

Chatterjee, A. K. *Use of Agricultural and Industrial Wastes in the Construction of Low-Cost Houses.* Kumasi, Ghana: Building and Road Research Institute, 1974.

Clark, John D. *Ignition! An Informal History of Liquid Rocket Propellants.* New Brunswick, N.J.: Rutgers University Press, 1972.

Eldridge, E. F. *Industrial Waste Treatment Practice.* New York: McGraw-Hill, 1942.

Farmer, Gary. *Unready Kilowatts: The High-Tension Politics of Ecology.* La Salle, Ill.: Open Court, 1975.

Feasibility of Utilizing Solid Wastes for Building Materials, Report EPA-600/8-77-006 and Supplement EPA-600/2-78-111. Washington, D.C.: Environmental Protection Agency, 1977 and 1978 (supp.).

Field Intelligence Agency Technical Reports (F.I.A.T. Reports). Military Government for Germany, U.S. 1945-1949.

Many of these reports were consulted in the preparation of Chapter 4. The most important are:

446   *Plastics, Moulded Plywood, and Adhesives in Aircraft Production.*
452   *Synthetic Wool Clothing.*
513   *Hydrogen and Methane Production from Coke Oven Gas.*
543   *Textile Research in Wartime Germany.*
552   *Fiberglass Fabrics for Defense Purposes.*
572   *Resin-Filled Fiberboard from Wood Chips.*
651   *Paper-Tube-Based Containers.*
673   *Various Unorthodox Engine Developments.*
755   *Highlights of the Iron and Steel Industry.*
795   *Uranium Compounds Produced from Pitchblende.*
888   *The Synthesis of Methanol at I. G. Farben.*
904   *High Voltage DC Transmission Over Long Distances.*
907   *The Re-refining of Scrap Aluminum from Crashed Aircraft.*
938   *The Gasification of Coal.*
952   *High Pressure Hydrogenation in Germany.*
1003   *The Chemical and Technical Basis for the Synthesis of Butadiene.*
1011   *The Fabrication of Aluminum in Germany.*
1035   *German Developments in High Explosives.*
1060   *Pumped Storage Power Plants in Germany.*
1111   *German Wind Turbine Projects During the Hitler Era.*

1119 *Methods of Transmitting 2 Megawatts for 600 Kilometers.*

1123 *The Precast Concrete Products Industry in Germany.*

1158 *War Experiences of the Berlin Power and Light Company (Bewag).*

1203 *Utilization of Oxygen in the German Iron and Steel Industry.*

1294 *Thermal Cracking of Ethane.*

1306 *Production of Wallboard and Wood Substitutes.*

Ford, James M., and James E. Monroe. *Living Systems: Principles and Relationships.* San Francisco: Harper & Row, Canfield Press, 1974.

Fuhrmann, Ernst. "The Long-Life Car." *Futures,* June 1979.

Hannon, Bruce M. "Bottles, Cans, Energy." *Environment,* March 1972.

Hannon, Bruce M., R. G. Stein, et al. *Energy Use for Building Construction.* Washington, D.C.: Department of Energy, 1977.

Hitte, Steven J. *Anaerobic Digestion of Solid Waste and Sewage Sludge to Methane.* Washington, D.C.: Environmental Protection Agency, 1976.

Indiana State Board of Health. *Proceedings of the First Industrial Waste Conference,* vol. 1. West Lafayette: Purdue University Press, 1944.

Hoffman, George A., *Automobiles — Today and Tomorrow.* Memorandum RM-2922-FF. California: The Rand Corp., 1962.

Ireland, Frank, ed. *The Cost of Coping with Lead in Petrol.* London: Fellowship of Engineering, 1980.

Keynes, John Maynard. *General Theory of Employment, Interest, and Money.* New York: Macmillan, 1936.

Knight, J. A., J. W. Tatom, et al. *Pyrolytic Conversion of Agricultural Wastes to Fuels.* Atlanta: Georgia Institute of Technology Press, 1974.

Ley, Willy, *Engineer's Dreams.* London: Scientific Books, 1956.

Look, Editors. *Oil for Victory: The Story of Petroleum in War and Peace.* New York: McGraw-Hill, 1946.

McCormac, B. M., ed. *Introduction to the Scientific Study of Atmospheric Pollution.* The Hague, Neth.: Reidel, 1971.

Meadows, D. H., D. L. Meadows, J. Randes, and W. E. Behrens. *The Limits of Growth.* New York: Universe, 1972.

Milward, Alan S. *The German Economy at War.* New York: Oxford University Press, 1965.

Minke, Dr.-Ing. Gernot. *Alternative Construction Technologies and Materials for Low-Cost Housing.* Kassel, West Germany: Technical University of Kassel, 1979.

Odum, Howard T. *Environment, Power, and Society.* New York: Wiley, 1971.

Porsche, Dr.-Ing. Ferry. *We at Porsche.* New York: Doubleday, 1976.

Pound, Arthur. *Industrial America.* Boston: Little, Brown, 1936.

Rabbit, Peter. *Drop City.* New York: Olympia, 1971.

Rybczynski, Witold M. *The Ecol Operation.* Montreal: Minimum Cost Housing Group, McGill University, 1972.

_____. "Sulphur Building." *Architectural Design,* December 1975.

_____. *Use It Again, Sam.* Montreal: Minimum Cost Housing Group, McGill University, 1975.

Scoville, Warren C. *Revolution in Glassmaking: Entrepreneurship and Technological Change in the American Industry 1880–1920.* Cambridge, Mass.: Harvard University Press, 1948.

Searl, Milton F., ed. *Energy Modeling: Art, Science, Practice.* Washington, D.C.: Resources for the Future Inc., 1973.

Shah, Kirtee. *The Unbalanced Equation.* Ahmedabad, India: Ahmedabad Action Study Group, 1977.

Staackmann, Milton, and Thomas C. Goodale. *Rice Hull Utilization.* San Mateo, Ca.: URS Research Company, 1970.

Talbot, Frederick A. *The Oil Conquest of the World.* Philadelphia: J. B. Lippincott, 1914.

Taylor, Theodore B., and Charles C. Humpstone. *The Restoration of the Earth.* New York: Harper & Row, 1973.

Ungewitter, Claus, ed. *Verwertung des Wertlosen* (Berlin, 1938). trans. L. A. Ferney and G. Haim, *Science and Salvage.* London: Crosby, Lockwood & Son Ltd., 1944.

Use of Agricultural and Industrial Wastes in Low-Cost Construction. United Nations Publication ST/ESA/51. New York: Center for Housing, Building, and Planning, Department of Economic and Social Affairs, 1976.

Williamson, Harold F., and Arnold R. Daum. *The American Petroleum Industry Vol. I: The Age of Illumination 1859–1899.* Evanston, Ill.: Northwestern University Press, 1959.

Wonen met Karton. Bindhoven, Netherlands: Stichting Architecten Research, 1974.

Illustration Credits

1. Clare Wheldon
2. Author
3. Author
4. Clare Wheldon
5. Clare Wheldon
6. Clare Wheldon
7. Clare Wheldon
8. Author
9. Clare Wheldon
10. Author
11. Clare Wheldon
12. Clare Wheldon
13. Clare Wheldon
14. Author/Jon Goodchild
15. Author/Jon Goodchild
16. Van Tassel*/Jon Goodchild
17. Adler*/Jon Goodchild
18. Adler*
19. Van Tassel*/Jon Goodchild
20. Bond, Straub*
21. Bond, Straub*/Jon Goodchild
22. Author/Jon Goodchild
23. Author
24. Ley*/Jon Goodchild
25. Ley*
26. Adler*
27. Hoffman*/Jon Goodchild
28. The Manx Museum
29. Author
30. Witold Rybczynski
31. Glass Container Corp.
32. Author
33. Author
34. Author
35. Michael Reynolds/Jon Goodchild
36. Author/Jon Goodchild

37. Reynolds Metals Company
38. Author
39. Morris Schopf
40. Sterling King
41. Masius, Wynne-Williams & D'Arcy MacManus
42. Author
43. Author
44. Terry Green
45. Reynolds Metals Company
46. Witold Rybczynski
47. Witold Rybczynski
48. Witold Rybczynski
49. Gernot Minke
50. Gernot Minke
51. Martin Chandler
52. Michael Reynolds
53. Michael Reynolds
54. Michael Reynolds
55. Larry Birch
56. Michael Reynolds
57. Michael Reynolds
58. Michael Reynolds
59. Larry Birch
60. Michael Reynolds
61. Michael Reynolds
62. Michael Reynolds
63. Clare Wheldon
64. Author
65. Clare Wheldon
66. Clare Wheldon
67. Tony Fernandez
68. Author
69. Author
70. Alan Wolfe
71. Author
72. *Building Design*

73. Author
74. Gernot Minke
75. Gernot Minke
76. Gernot Minke
77. Leonard Koren
78. Gernot Minke
79. Gernot Minke
80. Jeff Skorneck
81. Jeff Skorneck
82. Rinus van den berg/Jon Goodchild
83. Rinus van den berg
84. Rinus van den berg
85. Rinus van den berg
86. David Porter
87. David Porter
88. American Can Company
89. John Habraken
90. John Habraken
91. John Habraken
92. Porsche design office/Jon Goodchild
93. Porsche design office/Jon Goodchild
94. Porsche design office/Jon Goodchild
95. Porsche design office/Jon Goodchild
96. Author
97. Author
98. Author/Jon Goodchild
99. Author
100. Author
101. John Donat
102. Clare Wheldon

*Caption contains credit reference

Index

Agricultural wastes in U.S., 28–30, 30 (Table 5); construction potential of, 88, 90

Agriculture: intensive, 28–30, *illus. 29*; nonintensive, 28, *illus. 29*, 79

Airborne particulates, sources of in New York City, 24 (Table 2)

American Can Company, 5, 11, 19

American Cyanamid, 11

Americology plant, Milwaukee, 150

Architect's Research Institute (SAR), 115, 141, 143

ATIM/ATIP project, *illus. 142*, 143, 153

Beck, Robert, 9

Becker, Hollee, 15

Bender, Richard, 83

"Biological transformations," 151

Biotechnology, 150–151, 162

Black market, 175

Bottles, 13, 115, 133, 136–137, 138, 141, 143, 145 n.11, 152–154; structures made from, *illus. 89, illus. 136,* 137. *See also* ATIM/ATIP; Building; San Vitale

Bottle wall, *illus. 19*, 152–153

Bricolage, 109; in America, 109–110; in developing countries, 110, 112; Drop City dome, *illus. 110*; high technology example of, *illus. 113*

Bricoleurs, 175, 176–177

Building: for tomorrow, 167–182; with bottles, 153–154

Building codes, 7, 123

Building materials, 169–170, 175–176; waste-derived, 93–94. *See also* "Envirite;" "Glasphalt;" Glass (waste)

Buildings as energy storage, 101–105

Bus bodies, recycled in Chile, 121, 139

Campamento. See Chile

"Can block construction, *illus. 123, 124*, 125

Can house, 1, 5, *illus. 6*, 121, 129

"Can-laying," 11, 13

Cans, *illus. 8, 9*, 11, *illus. 12, 13, 115, 125, illus. 129;*

aluminum, 126, *illus. 126, illus. 130* (*See also* Energy analysis); beer, *illus. 111,* 112, 152–154 (*See also* WOBO); bimetal, 137, 145 n.13; clips for, *illus. 129,* secondary use of, *illus. 176*; steel, *illus. 125;* tin-free steel (TFS), 149–151. *See also* Oil drums

Car parts, 105 n.5, 105 n.6, 141, *illus. 142, 143, illus. 144*, 145 n.1. *See also* Bus bodies, Dome building

Cars, converted into emergency housing, 139, 141 (*See* Citroen Chilena SA project. *See also* Housing); secondary use of, *illus. 180*

Cellulose, 159–160; insulation plant, *illus. 159*

Chicago Sun-Times, 1

Chile, housing in, 177; *campamento, illus. 174*. *See also* Citroen Chilena SA project; ODEPLAN

Citroen Chilena SA project, 139, 141, *illus. 140, illus. 141–143*

Commodities, estimated world production of, 178

(Table 22)

"Concorde fallacy," 83

Concrete, 7, 9, *illus. 130*

Construction industry, deficiencies in, 172–173; consumer sector expanded for needs of, 173; in Chile, 177; in developing countries, 178; in the U.S., 178; in Third World, 176–177; worldwide failure of, 173–178

Consumer products, 83, 178

Consumer industries, as source for building materials, 175–176

Continental Can Company, 121, 125

Cornell University, 141

Counterculture, building in the, 109, 145 n.1

Crouch house, 5–20; construction of, 9; cost of, 20 n.3; design for, 7, 9; media response to, 11, 13, 14, 15; problems with, 15; *illus. 8, 9, 10, 12, 14, 15, 16, 17, 18, 19. See also* Sources of waste

Curtis house, 125, *illus. 126*

Van roof panels, *illus. 142*
von Richthofen, Manfred, 112

Waste, 1, 2, 5, 7, 47, 48, 50, 51, 79, 81, 91, 99, 100, 175, 179; in agriculture, 28–30; in America, 23–37; definition of, 36–37; 41–42, 46, 50; future of, 1, 35–37, 48–50; 165; in industry, 31–32; in mining, 25–27; municipal, 33–34; nature of, 39–54; of power in modern automobiles, *illus. 80*; projections for, 35–37; from steel pro-

duction, *illus. 32*; transformation of, 42–43; 44–47. *See* Leblanc process. *See also* Airborne particulates; Demolition waste; Gasoline; Germany; Household waste; Preconsumer wastes; Processed waste buildings; Resource storage; Sod cottage; Solid waste; Sources of waste; Sulfur
Waste building, in the Third World, 87–90
Waste construction, 2, 13; and energy economics,

85–105
"Waste frame," 123, 125, *illus. 125, 126. See also* Curtis house
Waste material, 5, 7, 13, 18, 101, 178; in construction, 20, 87, 97; generated in petroleum production, *illus. 45. See also* Bottles, Cans, Car parts, Glass, Newsprint cores, Steel strapping
Waste-producing industries in U.S., 31 (Table 6), 32
Watts Towers, 112
Weather, effect of on waste construction, 9, 11, 13, 15

Wheeler, Ed, 15
Wisconsin Electric Power Company, use of solid waste by, 78–79
Wolfe, Alan, 131, 134
WOBO (WOrld BOttle), *illus. 142, 152,* 152–154, *illus. 153,* 165 n.3
World Energy Conference, 73–74
Wood shingle on wood frame wall, *illus. 98. See also* Energy analysis
Wright, Millard, 130